Your people - an employer's guide to recruitment & selection

By Penny Hackett

Edited by Andrew Steeds

INVESTORS IN
PEOPLE UK

Published by Investors in People UK
7–10 Chandos Street
London W1M 9DE
Tel +44 (0)171 467 1900
Fax +44(0)171 636 2386
E-mail: information@iipuk.co.uk
Website: www.iipuk.co.uk

First published as *Choosing the Players* by the Institute of Personnel and Development in 1994

This edition first published 1999
Editor Andrew Steeds

Typesetting Creation Communication Design Limited

Cover design The Workroom

Printed and bound by Jarrold Book Printing

British Library Cataloguing in Publication Data

A catalogue record for this book is available from the British Library

ISBN 1–900567–06–7

contents

About this book

All businesses stand or fall on the quality of the people who work for them. Being able to identify what staff are required, and thereafter to set about recruiting them, are two crucial skills that are fundamental to business success. These skills are by no means straightforward, however, and for many small businesses in particular the process of identifying and filling job vacancies often appears fraught with problems.

Your People – an employer's guide to recruitment & selection is designed to explain this process as clearly as possible to anyone approaching the activity of recruitment for the first time – and, indeed, to anyone else who feels that their practice in this area could be improved. Each chapter discusses the various stages of recruitment and provides clear guidelines for behaviour and procedures, as well as drawing attention to constraints imposed by existing legislation.

A number of organisations are listed in the Useful Addresses section at the end of this book. This list is not intended to be exhaustive, and there will inevitably be other organisations that individual businesses need to contact. Addresses and telephone numbers of organisations listed are correct at the time of publication.

Your People – an employer's guide to recruitment & selection is part of the *Building a Better Business* range of materials, produced to meet the needs of smaller, developing organisations. Core to this range is a practical business development tool kit, which pulls together all the disciplines of good business management.

The books in the range have been produced as practical, self contained resources, which can be taken on their own or, used to supplement the individual sections from the tool kit.

All materials in the range are published by Investors in People UK.

1 **defining** the game

THE BASIC FUNCTIONS OF BUSINESS

In every business, there are three basic functions:

- manufacturing/service
- marketing
- accounting.

Manufacturing/service operations

Whatever business you are in, your company must have its own special product or service proposition. If you are not able to satisfy the wants of your present and future customers more quickly and/or less expensively and/or to a higher standard than your competitors, you will not be in business for long. Your manufacturing or service *operations* are at the core of your business.

Marketing

Unfortunately, it is not enough simply to be able to do these things. Unless enough people know you can do them, and are willing to buy what you have to sell at a price that enables you to keep on making a profit, your business will soon fail. Effective *marketing* of your business proposition is essential.

Accounting

Unless your business has a firm financial base, sound positive cash flow and prudent financial management, it will not succeed. So careful *accounting* is imperative.

THE RIGHT PEOPLE

All three of these business functions – accounting, marketing and operations – are vital for success. But they all hinge crucially on your having the right people:

- doing the right things
- in the right way
- at the right time
- in the right place
- at the right price.

Managing people effectively is the real key to business success – and business success is what you are in business for.

Each member of your team has their own talents. If you bring your team's players together in a way that enables each to make their own best contribution to a clear team objective, you have a winning combination. If, however, you fail to make use of their individual abilities and force them to work in ignorance of the real objective or of what they can do to help achieve it, then their performance is likely, at best, to fall well short of your business's full potential.

Getting the right team together is something you will need to start to think about as soon as your business becomes more than a one-person band. Later chapters will explore some of the ways in which you can organise the work and find the best people to do it. The focus in this chapter is on exploring the pros and cons of building a stable team of employees.

Of course, you may have decided that actually taking people on to your payroll is too complicated and, instead, you will sub-contract work to other firms or self-employed individuals. This, and a range of other options, will be explored in Chapter 2.

SHORT–TERM OR LONG–TERM CONTRACTS: WHICH IS BEST?

One option you have as an employer, or a potential employer, is never to employ anyone for more than a pre-determined length of time. This is best done by creating a fixed-term contract. If the fixed term is to be more than one year, you will need to ask your employees to sign away some of their legal rights.

At first sight this seems attractive. Among other things, it means that you can:

- part with people at the end of the contract without a redundancy payment;
- regularly review exactly what work needs to be done and what skills are needed to do it, recruiting new people with the right talent rather than incurring the expense of retraining the old ones;
- frequently bring in people with new ideas and ways of working, to challenge some of your assumptions – external stimulus of this kind can be very healthy for a business and prevent it stagnating.

The disadvantage of such flexibility can be instability and demotivation. It is hard to get the best out of people who have no long-term stake in the success of the business, and to do so requires considerable thought. Hiring the same person on a series of short-term contracts is no solution either: in certain circumstances, such contracts count towards continuity of employment and therefore give the employee the legal rights you are trying to avoid.

The cost of departing employees and new recruits

It is also worth remembering that, no matter how long they have worked there, every person who leaves your business takes away:

- the skills you have helped them develop;
- the knowledge of your business and business processes they have acquired;
- the contacts they have made while working for you.

They may now put all of this to use for one of your competitors.

Departing employees can also take away:

- odd bits of equipment, uniform, stationery and so on – it may not be worth trying to reclaim these, but they nevertheless represent a cost to the company and could be used to your detriment;

- the intangible contributions they have made to help your business to function – the person who organises the company's social events, or the one who knows how to take the tension out of difficult meetings with some well-timed humour, will be sorely missed, even if these qualities are not to be found in any formal job description.

And every new person who replaces a departing employee must:

- learn to apply their skills and knowledge in a new context, quite possibly with a boss and colleagues whose expectations of them differ from those of their previous employer;

- get to know their way around your business, its people, terminology, systems and methods of working;

- win acceptance from their colleagues and customers.

Even if your new employees don't need to acquire new knowledge and skills – and some certainly will – they will need to settle in and find their feet. This means they are unlikely to work to their full potential for the first few days, weeks or even months.

The perils of selecting the wrong person

Selecting new people to work with is not easy, and there is always the risk that you will pick someone who isn't right for your business. If you regularly recruit people on short-term contracts, the chances are you won't always get it right. If you get it wrong, and choose someone who hasn't got what it takes, then you will face other problems. For a start, you will have wasted time and money on recruitment and, perhaps, training. You will also have had days, weeks or months of sub-standard performance. This can be a double loss: you will have sacrificed necessary output, paying wages for little or no return; and the ill-chosen recruit may actually have antagonised customers, suppliers or colleagues through their incompetence. This will reflect badly on the business as a whole.

If you act too quickly to remedy the mistake by sacking the recruit, other employees may think you are being hasty or unfair. If you don't act quickly enough, they may resent having to carry a passenger. Whenever you do decide to sack the recruit, there will be the stress, for you and the employee, of parting. This may just be the sleepless night before you bite the bullet, but your ex-employee may create real difficulties for you – perhaps by alleging they have been dismissed on the grounds of pregnancy, race, sex or trade union activity. It is illegal to dismiss an employee, from the first day of their employment with you, for any of these reasons.

For all these reasons, it makes sense to try to create a measure of confidence and stability in your team.

The advantages of different arrangements for different sections

When you come to weigh up the pros and cons of stability versus flexibility for your business, you may find different sections yield different answers. There may be some areas in which stability will be beneficial – perhaps because of the complexity of the work involved or the need to build and maintain customer relations. In others, flexibility and new ideas may be vital to keep ahead of the competition.

Much will depend on the nature of the roles to be filled, which in turn depends on what your business does and how it is organised. So before looking in detail at the process of recruitment itself, it is worth considering some of the different ways in which the key roles in your team may be allocated.

PLANNING THE TEAM

Many small businesses develop around the skills and entrepreneurial instincts of just one or two people: indeed, many of the largest corporations started this way, too. At some point in their history, the founders recognised the need for help – the need to share the work with people – to enable the business to grow.

Sometimes it is easy to see what you need. Let's say the skills of the founder are all to do with technological innovation and product creation:they may readily recognise that it makes sense to concentrate on that and to bring in someone else to go out and market the product, keep the books and manage the people. If the founder's skills and interests are less specific, the answer may be less obvious.

How you approach the solution will depend on your current position. If you already have a number of specialists working for you, and/or if you have set up particular individuals or groups with a specific focus, you probably won't want to rethink the organisation from scratch. If, on the other hand, your current employees are versatile and adaptable, working at the same level on the same assortment of tasks, you might find the following questions provide a useful framework for beginning to think about how best to divide up the work of your company.

What are you in business for?

For most people, the answer to this question will involve making money, for themselves and any other shareholders. For some, the emphasis will be short term – so that they can make a quick killing and retire to the South of France. For others, it will include building a firm financial base to be passed on from one generation to the next.

For most, making money is probably not the *whole* answer. Becoming the best, being the first choice for customers, being at the leading edge of development in the industry, helping to make the world a safer, healthier or more exciting place, providing interest, employment or a sense of purpose for those involved, or just wanting to be your own boss – all these may be part of your company's reason for being. Whatever

7

the answer, it will have a major bearing on the way you choose to do business. In particular, it will affect the way you treat your customers, suppliers and employees. If you are in business for the long term, and want to get and keep loyal customers, you will need to plan your work in a way that best serves *their* needs, rather than what is administratively convenient for you.

What key *functions* must be carried out within your business?

This question is not the same as asking what jobs there are. In all businesses there are operational functions to do with designing and delivering goods or services. In a retail business, these functions will be concerned with buying stock for resale, merchandising the shop and serving customers. In a manufacturing or processing one, the functions will revolve around the design and development of the product, the purchase of raw materials, transforming these into the finished item, packing and perhaps transporting them. In a hotel, the purchase of food and other supplies, and the provision of housekeeping and catering services, would fall into this category.

To support these operations, a number of other functions are necessary. Drawing your products and services to the attention of potential customers and persuading them to buy can be drawn together under the general heading of sales and marketing. Ensuring that invoices are sent to customers, payment collected and banked, accounts kept, taxes and employees paid is part of the accounting function. You may also need to include other functions to do with: renting, heating, lighting, furnishing and maintaining your business premises, getting and keeping staff, and ensuring that the company fulfils its legal obligations.

Each of these functions requires some degree of record keeping and monitoring to enable results to be measured and improved. This in turn may mean that there are functions to be carried out involving computer systems design, programming, data collection and reporting.

Depending on the size and complexity of the company, you may decide to allocate each of these functions to a different person; you may decide who to allocate them to on the basis of the knowledge and skills of the people currently working in the business, rather than a more abstract analysis. Nevertheless, try to look at the options through the eyes of your customers as well as those of your employees. If your customers find themselves unable to follow the logic of who does what when dealing with you, it may be time for a rethink.

What are the key *processes*?

Your customers are not interested in the functions being carried out inside your business. Their only concern is what results from your activities. Most importantly, they either want the goods and services you produce, and are prepared to pay for them, or they do not. So how do you bind all the separate functions together to make sure your customers get what they want?

The answer is to think in terms of *processes*. Whatever other aims and objectives you may have, in reality your business is about transforming inputs into outputs. The inputs may include ideas, knowledge, skill, cash and physical materials. The outputs can be anything from a comfortable night's sleep (if you run a guest house), to a carrier bag full of groceries (if you run a shop), to an attractive and secure home (if you are a house builder).

The processes through which you convert inputs into outputs are the thread running through your business, the channels along which information, materials and other resources flow. If they are well designed and functioning, they will ensure your customers' wants are satisfied. If they are not, everyone in the business will have to spend a wasteful amount of time disentangling them.

A process that is working well will produce few, if any, mistakes or delays and will require little inspection or checking. A process that is working badly will create bottlenecks (piles of part–finished products, in-trays full of unprocessed invoices, long and unhappy queues at the check-out) or errors (rooms that are double-booked; under– or overcharging; burst carrier bags; a leaky roof etc).

While a few of these outcomes may be the result of human stupidity, most will be the inevitable consequence of processes that are unequal to the task. Unfortunately, you will not put things right simply trying harder: you will need to re-examine all the activities that make up the process, to see which parts of the system are at fault.

What do your customers want?

From the customer's point of view, the best process is one that works and one that requires the least effort from them.

One-stop shopping is the customer's ideal. For the business, this means just one person to manage and operate the process from start to finish; for the customer, it would mean just one person to contact for everything from placing an order, to checking progress, to negotiating settlement and arranging delivery. A completely integrated process of this kind means no functional specialisation for anyone; instead, flexible teams do whatever is necessary to satisfy their customers. How feasible this is will depend on the range of products or services supplied, the number and location of your customers, and of course the stability and skills of your workforce.

ORGANISING YOUR TEAM

Organising your business on a geographical or product basis

If you do decide you would like your customers to be treated in this way, and assuming that your business is big enough to require some form of division of labour, there are two main options you might consider – organisation on a *geographical* basis and organisation on a *product* basis:

ORGANISATION ON A GEOGRAPHICAL BASIS

Organisation on this basis could mean establishing a European operation, a North American one, one for the Far East and so on. Alternatively, it might just mean separate groups of people working to service customers in different local postal districts. The members of each team would then design, make and deliver all your products to their customers, and also be responsible for all the other functions identified so far. Provided your employees have the necessary skills, knowledge and systems to enable them to do all these things efficiently and effectively, your customers should be satisfied.

Such an approach demands a considerable amount of duplicated effort, with separate sales and marketing activities, separate production facilities, separate accounting. However, provided everyone works to clearly defined principles and procedures, this can be very effective in getting and keeping everyone close to the customer.

ORGANISATION ON A PRODUCT BASIS

Say you install both double glazing and conservatories. Although you may buy both products from the same suppliers, you may find that, in the main, you are selling them to different customers. It might make sense to have some people specialising in windows while others concentrate on conservatories.

This will still mean some duplication of functions, and will be more difficult to apply where the products you provide are really interrelated. If, for instance, you produce skimmed and semi-skimmed milk, various types of cream, and ice cream – each of which either creates or uses by-products from the other – you might find it hard to separate your production facilities in the same way.

Organising your business on a functional basis

Dividing your labour either geographically or by product becomes less viable the more complex your products and the more sophisticated the skills required to produce them. However talented your employees may be, they are unlikely to be equally good at all the specialist functions identified so far. It may make more sense, therefore, to have one member of the team marketing and selling all your products to all your customers, while another looks after design and manufacture, and a third keeps the accounts and looks after the administration – in other words, to go for *functional specialisation*.

If you opt for such functional specialisation you should be able to reap the benefits of increasing expertise in each of the three functional areas discussed above. To make it work, though, you will need to find some way of helping all three to keep their attention focused firmly on the customer. It is all too easy for those whose day-to-day contacts are primarily with their fellow employees to lose sight of what their customers really want. Before long, they may start developing systems and procedures that make their own lives easier while actually making things harder for your customers.

You can reduce the chances of this happening by making sure that everyone understands the total process, and your employees' part in it. As long as each person understands what outputs (in terms of information, ideas, components and product) they must provide within the business – and to whom, when and in what format – you can build an internal chain of customers to help link your functional specialists to the real (external) customer.

How many levels of management do you want?

Each of the functions discussed so far calls for different skills. Each also comprises a number of different skills: day-to-day practical skills; organisational skills; and planning skills.

Day–to–day practical skills

The skills of the person who makes and decorates the cakes, welds the metal, makes up the beds, fits the carpets or does whatever else your customers are paying for, are central to the business. They add value to the raw ingredients and transform them into something your customers want. In the service or support functions, the skills of the person who writes the publicity leaflet, enters the data, makes out the invoices, collects the debts, are fundamental.

Organisational skills

However good your cake maker is, if they run out of sugar, or find the oven is too small, your business will not function smoothly and your customers will not be satisfied. Similarly, if you haven't bought enough sheets, or the laundry hasn't washed and ironed them, the beds in your hotel or guest house will not be made up, and again your customers will suffer. These simple examples highlight things that can make the difference between delivering what your customers want, when they want it – and failing to do so.

The bigger and more complex your business gets, the more vital these organisational skills become and the more broadly you will need to exercise them. Unless you co–ordinate activities effectively between functions, you could end up in real difficulties.

Suppose, for example, your sales and marketing person is offered some advertising space at an attractive rate. Believing they are doing the best job for the company, they take it and go to town with a glossy advertisement for a product you can't make at present because the components are stuck at the docks or your storage or assembly facilities are inadequate. Instead of the expected boost in sales, all you will achieve is customer frustration. This is not a good basis for a successful business.

Planning skills

Vital though day-to-day organisation and co-ordination are, unless you (and your bank) are prepared to live from hand to mouth for ever, you must look to the future. In big organisations, entire departments are sometimes set up purely to advise the board on the future social, demographic, environmental, political and economic trends that may have a bearing on the company five or ten years hence – and on how best to respond to these.

In a small business, there is neither the time nor the need to attempt to be too sophisticated. Nevertheless, a bit of forward planning can help to avoid too much crisis management – which is at best pretty stressful, at worst yet another route to customer dissatisfaction.

Too much time spent on considering 'what if' or thinking 'maybe' will not be productive; too little attention to the future can be disastrous. Businesses fail, for example, when they assume the boom will last for ever, or when they fail to anticipate the change in pedestrian flow arising from the proposed re-siting of a car park, or the decline in passing trade when a new by-pass opens. By developing a strategy for future growth, taking account of likely changes, you are more likely still to be in business when the future comes.

Levels of activity

So, whether or not you feel the need to divide the work into separate functions or geographical or product sections, you may feel it advisable to divide it into separate *levels of activity*, corresponding to the three different elements outlined above. You could decide, for example, that the place for strategic planning is the board room, the place for hands-on practical work is the shop floor, and the intervening organisation and co-ordination should be done by supervisors and managers.

If you do decide this, you will, of course, be mirroring the structure of a lot of organisations, large and not so large. You may, however, be missing an opportunity. If you allow too much hierarchical demarcation, it will become self-sustaining, and you will be unable to adapt to changing circumstances.

If people on the shop floor are told they must wait for the manager to get things organised and tell them what to do, they will usually wait. But if you ask them to take responsibility for getting themselves organised and to tell you what help they need, they usually will.

If you make it clear that the only people who are allowed to think round here are the bosses, the rest of your employees will use their brains in other ways – as school governors, organising charity events or doing a host of other things that actually demand quite a lot of planning and organising – outside work. If, on the other hand, you make it clear that it's everyone's job to come up with ideas for improving the business, at least part of that thinking power will be available to carry you forward.

This approach is finally winning converts in the board rooms of even the largest companies. The days when big corporations had fifteen layers of management between the chairman and the shop-floor are, mercifully, over. If your business is small, with a relatively flat hierarchy, your best bet is to keep things that way. Resist the temptation to distance yourself from the real work and hence lose contact with what your business is about. But do make sure you are not so busy minding the store that you simply don't have time to plan or to take advantage of new business opportunities.

Whatever decisions you have already made with regard to the overall shape of your business, keep them under careful review. Don't wait until after your first heart attack to decide you need to share the burdens of management. And don't assume that the structure that worked when you and your team were new to the game is the only one that will work now.

2 how many players?

CALCULATING THE NUMBER OF WORKING HOURS AND FULL–TIME EQUIVALENTS

If you divided your company into three functions – operations, marketing, accounting – and employed just one person to do each at the three different levels identified in the last chapter – planning, organising, doing – you would have nine people doing nine completely different jobs.

In practice, this would be completely unworkable for most businesses. For one thing, unless your business process is highly automated, you will almost certainly need a higher proportion of hands-on operations people than of anyone else: these are the only people who really add value, not the financial planners or the marketing co–ordinators. For another, you may well find that one person can sensibly combine several different activities, across a number of functions.

So how do you decide how many people you need? There are no hard and fast rules to help you answer this question, but these few pointers may be helpful:

Think in 'working hours', not numbers of people, to start with. There is no need to assume that all jobs will take exactly 39 hours per week (or whatever is the norm for a full week's work in your industry – this is discussed later in this chapter)

Start by looking at the practical operations. How long does it take to bake each cake, service each room or produce each batch of output? Obviously there will be variations, but a reasonable estimate of the average will do as a guide. How many cakes do you sell in a month? How many guests do you have? Once you have multiplied one figure by the other, you know how many working hours of operational activity (direct labour) you need

Now consider the support functions. How many working hours of practical accounting, administration, advertising and so forth do you need per sale? This will probably be an even less precise calculation, but try to be as realistic as possible. If necessary, monitor the work for a while to try to get a feel for the time spent. Again, multiply the number of working hours per sale by the number of sales, and you have your support function (indirect) working hours

Add the direct and indirect working hours together and multiply by what you consider to be a reasonable hourly rate for such practical work, including employer's National Insurance contributions. Some guidance on how to calculate rates is given in Chapter 6; you may, of course, want to introduce a higher level of precision into your calculations by using different rates for work in different functions

Now you know what your operational pay bill is likely to be and you may not like the answer. If you don't, you have only three options: speed up your operations; reduce your hourly rates; or go out of business. If you try to do anything else, you are simply deluding yourself

If you have got this far, the next step is to take account of the working hours that will need to be devoted to planning and organising. Work at this level usually attracts a higher rate of pay, so you will need to adjust the hourly rate calculation accordingly

The working hours spent on these activities are also less likely to be related quite so directly to the level of sales, so you may find it easier to work on the basis of simple ratios. One way is to analyse where time goes at present, for the people you currently employ

You might find that for every eight hours on the shop floor, one hour goes on planning and organising. Or you might find something closer to a 1:1 ratio. Whatever it is, unless you can find ways of improving on it, you will need to build it into your calculations and multiply by the relevant hourly rate

By now you will have a feel for the total number of working hours you will need per week or per month, with a rough idea of how these are distributed between activities, and an even rougher idea of how much they will cost. If you are an optimist by nature, you will probably have undercooked the figures a bit, so it may be a good idea to round them up before proceeding.

The next step is to consider how many 'full-time equivalents' the figures represent. Don't take your own working pattern as a model here. Just because you are prepared to work twelve hours a day, seven days a week, 52 weeks of the year, do not assume everyone else is. You must take account of holidays, sickness and standard hours.

Holidays

From November 1999, anyone who has worked for an employer for more than thirteen weeks is entitled to a minimum of four weeks' leave per year, in accordance with the European Working Time Directive.

Sickness

Colds, flu and other mishaps will take their toll of even the most dedicated workforce. You will be very lucky to get away with fewer than five days' absence per person per year, and you might find it closer to fifteen.

Standard hours

For most of British industry, 35 to 40 hours represent a full working week. Hours worked beyond this usually attract premium rates of pay (overtime) and are therefore expensive; however, making extra use of the skills of those who are already experienced, and in place, can be a lot cheaper than recruiting extra hands at flat rates – especially if the peaks are relatively brief. There is a limit to what is sensible, though: if you expect too many hours for too long a period, you will find mistakes occurring through plain weariness. In most occupations, the maximum hours people may work are now restricted by law to 48 per week, with a minimum daily rest period for adults of 11 consecutive hours and weekly rest of 24 hours every 7 days.

WHAT ARE THE JOBS THAT NEED TO BE DONE?

Once you have clarified the functions and activities to be performed, and calculated the approximate numbers involved, you can start to define specific *jobs*. There is no such thing as a perfectly designed job: almost all have their areas of frustration, boredom or ambiguity. But some are intrinsically more 'do-able' than others. Here are a few guidelines:

- Try to strike a sensible balance between specialisation and variety. Up to a point, the more people focus on one activity, the better they get at doing it – but only up to a point. Inserting one particular type of bolt, or packing one particular type of carton, all day, every day, gets very boring – and boredom leads to mistakes. So aim to include a range of related activities in each job, and to ensure that no activity is repeated too frequently

- Try to include some tasks that are relatively routine and others that are more challenging, some that involve working with others as well as some that are done in isolation. In particular, make sure as many jobs as possible include at least some element of contact with your customers

- Wherever possible, let people see things through. This is usually better for the customer and is also much more rewarding for the individual. It may not, for example, always be possible for someone who bought a particular batch of material to make it up, load it on to the lorry, deliver and install the finished product – but it should be possible for them to have responsibility for checking the material's arrival in the store and for getting feedback from the operators about what it's like to work with

- In most small businesses, it is unlikely that anyone will be so far removed from the finished product that they don't know what you're in business for, but it is quite possible, for example, for someone working in a large hotel kitchen to lose sight of the fact that you are in business to delight your customers rather than merely to peel potatoes

- Take account of what happens elsewhere. If you are going to have to recruit new people from time to time, for replacement or for growth, this will be easier if the jobs in your company bear at least some resemblance to those available in other companies. If you are the only person in the district who needs a software engineer who can write advertising copy, prepare your company accounts and erect marquees, you may not find yourself spoilt for choice when you try to recruit.

WHAT ABOUT HOURS OF WORK?

Having established what the jobs are, and roughly how many working hours you need for each, you are now ready to give serious thought to patterns of work. The main options are:

- Hire freelance or self-employed workers when you need them. These people will not be on your payroll and they will be liable for their own National Insurance and Income Tax payments. Bear in mind, however, that, if they are not, or if they are working closely under your direction, you could find they are deemed in law to be your employees after all – see *Your People – an employers' guide to successful people management* for more discussion of this issue

- Hire *agency personnel*. You will find details of your local employment agencies in *Yellow Pages*. As well as helping you recruit your own employees, most agencies have a register of people who are retained by the agency but who will work for other employers on a temporary basis. Any contract of employment is normally with the agency rather than the person using their services

- Employ people on a *part-time* basis for a few hours per day or per week

- Employ people on a *fixed pattern* of hours, to correspond with those when you are open for business

- Employ people on *flexi-time* – i.e. agree the total number of hours to be worked in a month or a quarter, and the core time when all employees must be present (e.g. from 10.00 to 16.00). Leave employees to decide, individually or in work groups, what time they actually start and finish each day

- Employ people on an *annual hours* contract – i.e. agree the total number of hours they will work in a year, and the money they will get in return, and then call on them to work when you need them

- Employ people on a *shift basis* – either fixed or variable – to maximise machine usage, keep the process running, or service your customers around the clock

Any of the employment options can be entered into on a permanent, temporary or fixed-term basis. The pros and cons of non-permanent employment were discussed in Chapter 1 (see p. 2); fixed-term contracts for periods of more than two years will entitle employees to the same treatment as permanent employees with the same service, unless they explicitly agree to waive their right to claim unfair dismissal or a redundancy payment.

Each of the above options has its attractions, and you can use a combination for different roles. Which pattern you adopt will depend on your answer to a number of questions.

How much flexibility do you need?

If your business fluctuates widely at different times of the year, it will be simplest to hire freelance workers, go to an agency, or recruit your own temporary staff. There are, however, drawbacks:

- Legal responsibility. You will need to make sure the legal basis is clear. You don't want suddenly to find that the person you thought was paying their own National Insurance and tax bill is in fact legally your responsibility as an employee

- Cost. Agencies have their own overhead costs to support, as, to a lesser extent, do the self-employed. Their hourly rates are likely to be higher than you would pay for your own employees

- Skill level. If your work is specialised, you may find it takes too long to get an occasional freelance or temporary employee to perform to the required standard

- Acclimatisation problems, of the kind discussed in Chapter 1, are likely to occur.

The next most flexible alternative, and one which overcomes the above problems, is the annual hours contract. Since you do not have to agree in advance exactly how the hours will be distributed, you can go some way to matching the available working hours to the peaks and troughs in your business, while ensuring you always have experienced people on hand when you need them. The drawbacks here are:

- Although you do not need to bring people in when there is no work for them to do, you will be paying them a constant amount throughout the year. The saving you make is in not having to pay premium rates for extra hours, or guaranteeing pay for short time

- Setting up such a contract is rather more complex than a standard hours arrangement, as both parties need adequate safeguards to avoid exploitation.

How many people do you want to be able to call on?

If there are just one or two real peaks in the year when you need lots of highly skilled people on hand, having plenty of part-timers on the payroll could be the answer: between them they will keep your business staffed throughout the year. When you really need everyone on hand, you can bring them all in at once – they will already be experienced and will not have got stale through working eight hours a day, day in day out.

There is a further advantage to using part-timers. To avoid claims of discrimination you must offer them *pro rata* the same pay and conditions as a full-timer, but you may save on National Insurance contributions. The percentage of employee earnings you must contribute increases as the employee's weekly earnings rise. For those whose earnings fall below the lower limit (£64 per week for 1998–99) you need pay nothing.

The main drawback is that not everyone wants to work part time. Most breadwinners need full-time earnings to make ends meet. An increasing number of employees are putting together their own portfolio of part-time work or becoming self-employed and working freelance, but they are still a minority. If you can only offer a few hours' work each week, it may not always be possible to recruit people with the skills and experience you need. One solution might be to share them with one or more other employers (even including your competitors), but they may then not be available to work extra hours for you as and when you need them.

What is the nature of your business?

Your customers' expectations may dictate a particular pattern. The hotelier who wishes to cater to his guests' every need must have staff on hand at midnight as well as at 06.00. If you must be operational 24 hours a day, shifts will be the answer. You can still use freelance or agency personnel to work shifts, but you may feel more secure establishing a regular team of your own people whom you know you can trust to work through the night without the same level of regular supervision as during the day.

Most people will expect to earn more for working anti-social hours, which will put up your costs, but this can be offset by the benefits of keeping expensive equipment fully used. It can certainly make sense to keep one machine working for 24 hours a day, rather than having three standing idle for a total of 48.

Opinions vary as to whether it is better to ask people to work fixed or variable shifts. In view of the difficulties of adjusting sleeping patterns, a permanent night shift appeals to some. Others prefer variety – three nights on, three off, followed by three days on, three off, followed by three evenings, and so on. If you do set up a shift system, you will need to think carefully about how you communicate with, and maintain the involvement and loyalty of, all three or four shifts. You will also need to consider how you make sure the same work standards are applied throughout.

What are your employees' needs?

Flexi-time can be particularly beneficial in crowded urban areas, where staggering starting and finishing times can save the amount of time employees spend travelling to and from work. It can also reduce the amount of lateness and absenteeism by enabling people to attend to family business, go to the dentist and so on outside core working hours.

SUMMARY

These first two chapters will have helped you think about:

- how to divide up the work – by function, geography or product;
- how many levels you need to cover the planning, organising and practical doing of the work;
- how many hours of work need to be done;
- how many people you would need, allowing for sickness, holidays and so on, and assuming everyone worked full time;
- how to group tasks together to form specific and worthwhile jobs;
- whether you want to employ everyone for eight hours a day, five days a week, or whether you choose to adopt some other pattern of work that better suits the needs of your customers, your employees and your business.

The next chapter assumes that you have resolved these issues, and that you now have at least one job for which you need to recruit.

getting **ready** 3

THE IMPORTANCE OF GETTING IT RIGHT

If your business has up to now been a one-person band or a family concern, you may never have had to think about recruiting a complete stranger to join your team. And even if you have already done some recruiting, you may well feel nervous at the prospect.

Whatever the basis of their employment with you, the people you recruit now will soon be 'insiders'. They will have access to at least some of your business secrets and ways of working. They may well see more of you than your family does.

For these reasons, as well as those discussed in Chapter 1, getting it right could be critical to the future success of your business. In a large company, one selection error is unlikely to prove fatal; in a small business, it just might.

ANALYSING THE JOB

It is worth investing some time in planning your recruitment – not just to reduce the risk of errors but also to increase the chances that your new recruit really will help your business to flourish.

Subsequent chapters will look in detail at where and how you can attract the right candidate, and how to make sure you choose someone who will be an asset to the team. As a first step, this chapter focuses on what you must do in order to increase your chances of success.

Unless and until you know precisely what you are looking for, you are likely to waste time, and possibly money, going up blind alleys. Your first two vital tasks are, therefore, to describe the job and to work out what it takes, in terms of the skills, knowledge and abilities to do it effectively.

Before you can do either, you will need to undertake some additional investigation to help you analyse what is required. This will differ depending on whether you are recruiting for a new job or an existing one.

Recruiting for an existing job

If you are recruiting for an existing job you will have two very useful inputs to your analysis. You can talk to the person who did the job before or to those who are already doing it. And you can talk to the people, inside and outside the business, who are their customers.

Interviewing the current job holder

The purpose of your conversation with the job holder will be to find answers to the following kinds of question.

- What *tasks* do they undertake, and what are the *skills* and *knowledge* that they most frequently use? This will help you work out what knowledge and skills to look for in the new recruit. The simple way to find this out is to ask the job holder to talk you through a typical day, week or month. Another option is to ask them to tell you about the key processes in which they play a part, and to help you identify the actions required. For more complex jobs, a third possibility is to see if they can keep a special log book or diary for a little while, to record their activities. If this is impractical, perhaps someone else could shadow them for a few days to observe what is involved

- What are the *frustrations* and *satisfactions* of the job? Knowing these can help you find ways of reducing the former, or at least forewarning potential recruits

- What sort of things does the job holder believe could be done to increase the *effectiveness of the job*? This will enable you to re-examine the job and see how it fits with other jobs in the company

• What are their *reasons* for going (if the job holder is leaving)? These may give you an insight into how it feels to work for the company, and help you form a view of the kind of people who are most likely to fit in and enjoy it. It won't always be appropriate to try to persuade them to stay. Unless you really have been seriously underpaying, overworking or otherwise mistreating them and can and will do better in future, it is sometimes best to leave well alone. Once people have made up their minds that the grass is greener somewhere else, it is best to let them go. If, as often happens, they find after a while that the old firm wasn't so bad after all, they'll be back. If you try to talk them out of finding out for themselves, they may always regret it and you may find yourself beginning to doubt their loyalty.

Keep a note of the key points that emerge from these questions, bearing in mind that your aim is to get enough information to help you decide what the job is all about and what it takes to do it well.

Interviewing customers and colleagues

The purpose of these conversation will be to find the answers to the following kinds of question:

• Where does the job fit in? What part does it play in the total business process? How does it contribute to the satisfaction of your customers' desires? What would happen if it wasn't there? Who would suffer? How? How else could their needs be met? Just occasionally you may find that the answers to these questions indicate that no replacement is needed after all. Usually they will help you to understand more about the critical elements of the job, the key tasks that must be carried out

• What are the attributes that other people value in previous or existing job holders? By asking for examples of the sorts of thing they do that work well, and of things that do not work so well, you will begin to build up a picture of what is needed. If, for instance, colleagues point out that mistakes in paperwork make their lives difficult, then attention to detail is clearly important in the job. If you press them to tell you the sort of mistakes that occur most frequently, you may establish that arithmetic errors are the real problem. From that you can deduce that you need someone who has the numerical skills to cope with the kind of calculations involved

- Try to make sure each conversation focuses on the positive as well as the negative. It is all too easy to concentrate exclusively on the things the previous job holder lacked when it comes to looking for a replacement. The *purpose* of these discussions is to help you analyse what you need next time around. In the example just given, unless you also discover that the person really helps customers to understand the product and its benefits, by explaining and demonstrating them clearly and patiently, you might recruit someone who is a mathematical genius but a lousy sales representative.

Listening carefully to the comments and ideas of the job holder, and of those who are part of the same process, will almost always provide a wider and deeper insight into both the job itself and the attributes required. It will also enable you to rethink the combination of tasks that go to make up the job before you start recruiting, if it is necessary to do so.

Recruiting for a new job

Identifying a weak link in your business process is the first step towards recruiting for a new job. You realise that somewhere along the chain from product design to customer, or in one of the supporting functions, something is missing. Maybe the relevant tasks are being carried out by someone as part of a bigger job; maybe they are spread around a number of people, with no one having real responsibility for seeing them through; maybe you have suddenly realised that there is a whole function that hasn't been happening. Whatever the reason, there is a gap that needs to be filled.

Your primary focus must be on the nature of that gap. Talk to people on either side of it: those who are producing output that would logically pass to the person filling the gap, and those who would use the output produced by the same person. You will ask the same sort of questions as those outlined above in relation to filling existing jobs. The difference will be that people will have to use a bit more imagination and think a bit harder about their answers.

Once they have given you the information you need, you can start to think about drawing up an outline of what you will want the new person to do.

DESCRIBING THE JOB

The last thing you want in a small, dynamic but (you hope!) growing company is a pile of paperwork – especially if the contents are likely to become set in concrete. Many large organisations have paid the price of taking too bureaucratic an approach to drawing up job descriptions. They have found themselves growing increasingly inflexible and suffered repeated demarcation debates as employees decided to do only what was written down.

You don't need a six-page document to describe each job. However, you do need a simple checklist to help you make sure you don't leave out anything important when you are talking to potential applicants or when you are trying to analyse the skills and knowledge needed to do the job.

Your checklist should include the following:

Title
You will probably want to use this in your advertisement or recruitment notice, so it should clearly convey the nature of the job. Some companies use fancy titles like 'customer service executive' when they mean 'sales assistant'. This may make those already doing the job feel good, but it can be very confusing for applicants.

Purpose
Note down the main reason why the job exists. Is it 'to drive the van'? Or is it 'to

deliver consignments of finished goods, on time and undamaged, to customers throughout south–east England'? The latter gives a clearer idea of the real responsibilities of the driver.

Key tasks

You don't need a detailed list of everything the job holder will do. 'Tidy the paper clips and the envelopes, count the pencils and order more paper' goes into too much detail. 'Run the office' is too general. 'Manage the stationery, provide a word processing/typing service for three people, set up and maintain the customer filing system (currently 150 customers) and route incoming mail and telephone calls to the appropriate person (currently 10 staff)' is probably as much detail as you would need to record for someone coming to help out in the office. You probably won't need to be reminded of the numbers, but most applicants like to get a feel of the size and scope of the job, and how busy they will be.

Conditions

Hours and days of work, rate of pay, and particular circumstances such as a requirement to travel or spend nights away from home, outdoor or particularly noisy or hazardous work, should all be noted down. These details won't necessarily go in the advertisement, but you must make sure you explain them at some stage – or you may find your new employee doesn't last very long (see Chapter 6 for further discussion of this issue).

Keep it simple, and to the point. Make sure you have covered all the issues raised in your discussions with previous or existing job holders. Don't be tempted to leave out tasks that you know are frustrating or difficult: not everyone will find them so, and your new recruit will not thank you for sweeping them under the carpet.

WORKING OUT WHAT YOU ARE LOOKING FOR

If you don't know what you're looking for, you have very little chance of finding it. It is tempting to skip this stage, in the belief that you will recognise it when you see it.

If you do this, however, it is more likely that you will fall for the most plausible and personable candidate – not the one with the skills and knowledge needed in the job.

So how do you translate your list of key tasks into a list of the skills and knowledge required for the position? One solution is not to try. If you want someone to manage your stationery, look for someone who has done it before somewhere else. If you want someone to do your word processing, look for someone who has a college certificate saying they have passed an exam in it.

This is certainly the quickest and easiest route and lends itself readily to conversion to a clearly worded advertisement or recruitment notice. This approach does carry a number of risks, however.

- Having done the same kind of work before does not necessarily mean that it has been done well or at the right speed to make it cost effective. You need to be clear what that standard is, and how you will recognise it when you see it

- Having passed an exam in something does not necessarily mean that the standard achieved will automatically transfer to the work-bench, shop or office. Even the fact that many qualifications are now linked to an assessment of competence through the system of National Vocational Qualifications (NVQs) is not a complete guarantee: a candidate may have good word-processing skills when using the local college software but be unable to transfer these same skills to the software you use

- Candidates with *identical* experience may not be attracted unless you have something extra to offer, for example pay, conditions, travel, location, or future prospects

- By insisting on previous experience you may rule out people who might very quickly master the work involved and end up doing it better than some of the experienced applicants. A classic example is the 'housewife' who wants to return to work and who may have experience of a whole host of activities, from taxi-driving to budgetary control, planning and organising others. If you are only prepared to consider applicants with a relevant employment record, you could miss out.

For all these reasons, it is better to take at least a little time to analyse what you really need. Must your driver have an HGV licence and no endorsements? Will you expect them to maintain the vehicle? If so, what will they need to know to do so safely? How much physical strength will be needed? What will happen if they get lost or are rude to your customers? What other skills are needed?

How important is it that your sales representatives not only are able to calculate discounts on the spot but are also familiar with all the technical features and functional benefits that customers will look for in your product? Must your receptionist be equally skilled in operating a particular type of switchboard (without losing calls) and pacifying irate callers when you are all out?

If you have spent time researching the job and its demands, it will be much easier for you to answer questions like these. Beware, however, of the danger of cloning, regardless of how good the previous job holder and/or existing employees might be. While you are unlikely to make a serious error if you look for someone with the same sort of background, education, experience and approach to life as the last holder of the job, you may not find anyone who *quite* matches. Even if you do, you may have missed the chance to bring in a really fresh set of ideas.

If the job you are trying to fill is really important to the future success of your business, it may be worth seeking help in identifying what you are after. There are a number of professional consultants who can help you to draw up a detailed profile of the behaviour, or the personality and other attributes, of the kind of person you need.

For the most part, however, all you will need to do is to approach the task in a reasonably systematic way, perhaps using an employee specification as a helpful framework. You can compile one by answering the following questions.

An employee specification

Do you need someone who:

- has specific technical, legal, financial or other knowledge?

- has knowledge or skill in operating or managing particular machines, processes, systems or procedures?

- has a particular level of physical strength or fitness, of manual dexterity or speed of thought? (Where or how will this be applied? How sure are you that someone who *hasn't* got these qualities would not be able to do the job some other way?)

- is good with figures? (What sort of calculations will they need to make, from what sort of information, with what sort of equipment?

- is good at making decisions? (What sort of decisions will they need to make, in what time-scales, with what input, and what consequences?)

- gets the best out of other people? (In what context will these skills be needed: individually or in groups? Using what sort of approach: dictatorial or consultative, telling or coaching?)

- always sees a job through? (What sort of jobs, in what time-scales, with what resources?)

- is good with words? (Does this involve reading or writing, letters, technical reports, advertising copy or other documents? Speaking or listening, presentations or less formal encounters?)

- plans and organises and prioritises? (Will this apply to their own work or other people's? How complex, in what time-scales?)

- has creative ideas? (About what, how often, how practical?)

- works well within a system and/or likes to know the rules and keep to them?

- is comfortable with uncertainty or ambiguity?

- is quick to learn? (What sort of things will they need to learn – technical, practical, theoretical? How – by doing, reading, observing?)

- is able and willing to drive? (What sort of vehicle will they have to drive, how far, how frequently, to what standard?)

- is able and willing to stay away from home? (How often will they need to do this, for how long, with what level of contact?)

- is able and willing to work on their own, making their own decisions and getting on with the job?

- shares the same values and general outlook as you have in so far as these relate to work and relationships with customers and colleagues?

- is flexible as regards working hours?

Avoiding discrimination in your recruitment advertisement

Once you have answers to all these questions, you have a template against which to measure candidates. This will help you to rule out any possibility of your prejudices getting the better of you. You are not looking for a superman or superwoman, black or white. You are looking for a *person* who matches the template. This is important. Regardless of how many employees you have, it is illegal to discriminate on the grounds of sex, marital status, race or ethnic origin. If you have more than fifteen employees, it is also illegal to discriminate on the grounds of disability. Unjustifiably specifying a requirement that is less likely to be met by members of a particular group can discriminate indirectly. The more systematic and objective you have been, the better.

With this template, you will also be able to draft a recruitment notice or advertisement specific enough to attract people with the right attributes, and to deter those without.

You are now ready to begin your search for someone to fill the gap in your team.

attracting **talented people** 4

RECRUITING FROM INSIDE YOUR COMPANY

The first place to look for someone to take on new responsibilities is inside your existing team. This may sound obvious, but it is surprising how often employees get 'pigeon-holed' into what they are doing at the moment. Just because you have only ever seen an employee performing one particular task doesn't mean they aren't capable of doing a completely different set of tasks, if entrusted to do so.

It might seem that this piece of advice should have come before the previous chapter's discussion of defining the job and what it takes to do it well – presumably you wouldn't need to do that if the solution to your recruitment problem was staring you in the face? In fact, the disciplines outlined in the previous chapter are equally important, whether you are recruiting from inside your business or outside it. It is all too easy, for example, to turn a perfectly competent van driver into a totally incompetent sales representative. Once you have done so, you and your employee are both losers: you, because you will probably end up with no van driver and no sales rep; the employee, because they will not only have lost their job but probably their self-esteem into the bargain.

You will only be in a position to match the skills and knowledge of your existing employees against your checklist if you work through the process of systematically determining what you need. If you do find a good match from within your business, everyone gains. Even if you have to replace them in their old job, you may well find it easier to find someone capable of relatively less-skilled tasks.

You will certainly find it an advantage to have someone in the new job who already knows their way around the company – for all the reasons discussed in Chapter 1. In the process, you may also be holding on to someone you would otherwise have lost. If someone is not given the promotion they are looking for within your business, it might only be a matter of time before you lose them. Once promoted, they have the chance to broaden their skills, experience more variety, and perhaps take more responsibility and a pay rise.

Spreading the word within the company

So, your first option when you have a job to fill is to look inside the company. Don't take it for granted that no one will be interested. Let people know there is a job to be filled and what you are looking for.

You can do this casually and informally when you are talking to people about other things: the grapevine will usually do the rest. As long as you let it be known that you are prepared to discuss the position with anyone who thinks they would like to be considered, you may be surprised at who comes forward.

If you are not in daily contact with everyone, you may need to resort to slightly more formal means – for example, a brief note for general circulation, or to go on a noticeboard. Even if no one actually asks to be considered, at least you won't have kept anyone in the dark about your plans.

If someone does express interest, neither you nor they should assume that the job is theirs for the asking. You will both need to spend time assessing whether the move really is to your mutual benefit – Chapter 5 has more advice on this process.

If it turns out that this is not a good move, for whatever reason, you need to make sure your employee understands why. If you appear to be turning down good applicants without proper thought, they (and their colleagues) will think twice about putting themselves forward again, and may even become disenchanted with their present job.

SEVEN OPTIONS FOR RECRUITING FROM OUTSIDE YOUR COMPANY

If you can't promote or transfer an existing employee, you have a number of other options. Which you use will depend on the nature of the job to be filled, the current state of the job market and, of course, how much you are prepared to spend. These options will be considered in turn, starting with the least expensive.

Word of mouth

Even if they are not interested in, or capable of doing, the job themselves, your present team may know someone who is. Encouraging them to talk to friends and relatives can be a very cost-effective way of attracting new recruits. It can be used for any type of work and is quick and easy. Some employers believe in it so strongly they even offer a bonus to existing staff who introduce someone who stays for a specified period.

There are three major pitfalls, all of which can be avoided with a bit of common sense. These are a lack of variety, objectivity or productivity.

Lack of variety

If all your present employees come from the same sort of background, you will miss the chance to bring in someone different. This could be a problem: if, for example, your employees are all white males, and their circle of friends and acquaintances is also white and male, there is a chance you're missing out on the benefits of a multi-racial, mixed-gender workforce.

Your company may be too small to warrant much attention from the Commission for Racial Equality or the Equal Opportunities Commission (which help to uphold the law against race and sex discrimination). But both recommend that your choice of recruitment sources should be geared to attracting suitably qualified applicants from as wide a cross-section of the community as possible.

Lack of objectivity

If someone whom you value highly recommends a close friend or relative, you may be tempted to say 'yes' without really analysing whether they are capable of doing the job to the standard you require. Once you have asked for recommendations, you need to be careful that you and the present employee understand that there is no obligation, and no reflection on your employee, if you decide not to follow their recommendation.

Lack of productivity

If you do recruit someone on this basis, you need to be aware that 'keeping it all in the family' isn't always a good idea. People recruited in this way can work very effectively together. Indeed, their shared involvement may mean they feel a higher level of commitment and loyalty to the business than either of them would on their own.

But there are risks, especially if the two of them work directly together and without close supervision; in such circumstances, it can be all too easy to turn a blind eye to each other's minor, or even major, lapses. At the extreme, they may even decide to work together against the business, systematically defrauding you.

Such cases are rare, and shouldn't deter you from sensible use of word-of-mouth recruitment. They should, however, be mentally noted and encourage you to avoid putting temptation in people's way.

The Job Centre

Recruiting from the Job Centre costs nothing. There is one in nearly every town, and you will find the address of your local one in the telephone directory under 'Employment'. The staff are trained to help you define what it is you are looking for and to put you in touch with people who may be suitable. Whether you are looking for skilled or unskilled workers, this is a good place to start, the only real disadvantage being that you may find you get too many applicants who have not been properly vetted by the Job Centre.

Training packages for the unemployed

Many of those applying from the Job Centre are likely to be unemployed. There may be a particular advantage in taking on someone who has been unemployed for long enough to qualify for the New Deal. You could offer a training placement rather than permanent employment, which means you provide a chance to learn, while the government supports part or all of the cost.

You may feel that the knowledge and skills you are looking for are more likely to be found in someone who is currently working – perhaps for one of your competitors. Even so, it will be worth talking to the Job Centre, making it clear that you are not prepared to see just anybody who thinks they'd like an interview. You have nothing to lose by having your vacancy on their noticeboard at the same time as you are pursuing other avenues.

The Careers Office

If you are happy to take someone straight from school and train them up, contact the local Careers Service. Provided you are prepared to release them for the necessary off-the-job training and can give them a reasonable opportunity to learn on the job and to achieve NVQ Level 3, you could find the Modern Apprenticeship Scheme a cost-effective solution.

Local colleges

If you need someone with a specific qualification, there may be no need to look further than your local college of further education. Most run courses on a very wide range of subjects, ranging from building trades to hairdressing, and from motor mechanics to computer studies. Many of these help to develop very practical skills, and are again linked to NVQs. Most attract some more mature students, as well as school leavers. A telephone call to their careers office should get you on the right track.

If there is a university near you, you may be able to recruit someone with more advanced qualifications. Ask their careers officer whether courses include a placement period: you may be able to get someone in temporarily on this basis. If you need a permanent recruit, you can be sure that graduates of such programmes have at least a little practical experience as well as their theoretical knowledge.

Should you think someone like that would be too high-powered for your small business, remember that over 30 per cent of school leavers now go on to higher education. If you need someone with a bit of thinking power and the ability to learn, you ought not to discount this as an entry route these days – especially if you recruit from a relevant vocational course.

Gate, doorway and window notices

These notices can be effective and need not be expensive. A tatty piece of cardboard stuck out in the wind and rain at the entrance to your premises may not have much impact. But a carefully worded, professional-looking board – perhaps at the entrance to the industrial estate or business park, or in your shop window or office doorway – can be useful, especially for casual or unskilled labour. You are not likely to find a qualified accountant by this route, but you might well find shop-floor workers or a driver.

These notices are easy and cheap to produce with current DTP and word-processing packages. They may also be prepared with letters on a magnetic board, or as a series of carefully written cards (ideally encapsulated in film) for outdoor use. They vary from the unspecific 'Help Wanted' to a more precise list of job titles for current vacancies. The drawback is that you have no way of sifting applicants – and you probably won't be able to put enough information on the board to encourage self-selection. So you will need to have someone on hand to respond to the enquiries of passers-by.

The person you appoint to do that must have at least a little training. Not only should they be familiar with the job on offer and the skills required, they must also be careful not to say anything that might be construed as sex, race or disability discrimination. The person who thoughtlessly tells a female enquirer 'Oh no, that's a man's job', or who turns away enquirers from particular ethnic groups, could land you with a claim for sex or race discrimination. If you lose, it could cost you thousands of pounds.

Advertising

You can advertise in a bewildering array of publications, or on local radio or TV. All will charge you for the privilege – at rates varying from a few pounds to several thousand. If you have only one or two vacancies to fill, national newspapers and radio or TV are generally too expensive to consider, and in most instances you will find the local paper does the job more effectively. Unless you are prepared to pay relocation expenses, it's probably best to restrict your advertising to the local area anyway.

If you need people with particular skills, though – a food technologist, a software engineer, a quantity surveyor – it is worth searching out the relevant specialist periodical. You will find current information on such publications in *British Rate and Data*. This gives addresses, circulation details, advertising rates and so on. You should be able to find an up-to-date copy in your local reference library. If you advertise in these specialist periodicals, be prepared for the inevitable questions about relocation, though, as most of these publications have a national circulation.

Checklist for preparing advertisements

Should you write it yourself or employ an advertising agency?

Employing an advertising agency need not be a lot more expensive than writing the advertisement yourself, as most of their revenue will come in the form of commission from the publication where the advertisement is placed.

If you have used an agency to help you with product advertising, don't assume they will be the best choice for recruitment: the skills are different, and an agency that specialises in recruitment work is more likely to be able to give you sound advice on where to place the advertisement. Most agents will have an entry in *Yellow Pages*, but you may do better to ask around locally.

Most agencies will provide you with artwork of the advertisement for you to send straight to the periodical. If you decide to write the advertisement yourself, you will find that many periodicals will take your word-processed or DTP version and simply organise the page layout for you.

What should you say?

You can only answer this by bearing in mind the main purpose of the advertisement: that is, to enable the person who has the skills and knowledge you seek to recognise themselves and feel sufficiently attracted to the job to apply. You really don't want hundreds of applications. You only need one, so long as it's the right one.

Put yourself in the candidate's shoes. What do they need to know in order to decide whether to apply? (The job description and employee specification should help you.) Look at the list below for a few do's and don'ts.

For a relatively simple advertisement that you want the paper to typeset for you, it is enough to write or type the text clearly – or even phone it through. Anything more elaborate may require professional typesetting, together with graphics from a marketing or advertising agency or graphic designer. They will pass the necessary images on to the newspaper in the appropriate format – for a fee.

What sort of advertisement should it be – classified or display?

Classified or 'small ads' are cheap but generally uninviting. Only those seriously looking for a move bother to study them closely. You can try to make yours stand out by spreading out the text, varying the type size and creating a bit of space within the column. For relatively unskilled jobs that you haven't been able to fill by other means, this may be the best bet.

For more specialist positions, it may be worth investing in a larger, display advertisement. These give you a chance to section off part of the page, and be more creative in your presentation.

Drawing up an advertisement: some DOS and DON'TS

Do

- Make sure the job title is explicit. Put it in the headline, in large type.

- Specify what you are prepared to pay. This need not be an exact amount – top and bottom limits, or 'negotiable circa £200 per week', are much better than 'salary according to age and experience'

- Give as much information as you can about what the job entails. If the title is truly self-explanatory you needn't go into too much detail, but you must make sure candidates can see how they would spend their time. This is where your care in defining the job (Chapter 3) will pay off

- Make it clear what specific skills, knowledge and experience you require. You needn't include the whole list, but be sure to spell out clearly any that are essential.

- Give your company's name and address and a few words about the nature of your business. Include only enough information to enable applicants to see the job in some kind of context. Overselling the company, or padding out the advertisement by waxing lyrical about its achievements, isn't usually necessary

- Make it clear how, when and to whom the application should be made (see below)

- Try to write in a style that reflects the style of the company. Unless you are very formal in your dealings with employees, use 'you' and 'we', not 'the successful candidate' and 'the company'.

Don't

- Try to make the job or the company sound more glamorous than it is. It is a waste of your time to bring candidates along for interview under false pretences

- Say anything that could amount to sex or race discrimination. Job titles like 'manageress', 'storeman' or 'Girl Friday' come into this category, as do references to the successful candidate as 'he' (or 'she')

- Use two words where one will do. It will cost you more, and candidates will get bored

- Try to be too gimmicky. A professional advertising agency may be able to produce an eye-catching headline or graphic. Amateur efforts often end up embarrassing their originators and putting off candidates.

Using an employment agency

Advertising can be hard work. Not only do you have to spend time creating and/or vetting the advertisement and deciding where to put it, but there is also no certainty that it will produce the right response. If it attracts too many replies, you will spend hours sifting through them. If it doesn't produce the right sort, you will be back where you started – paying for yet another advertisement with no guarantee of success.

One way of avoiding this is to let a recruitment agency do the work for you. Although some agencies prefer to build up a relationship with companies that recruit regularly, others will be interested in 'one-offs'. Some specialise in particular types of job – computer personnel, drivers and fork-lift truck operators, secretarial or catering. Others offer a more general service – on either a permanent or temporary basis. You can find them listed in *Yellow Pages*, though recommendations through your business contacts may be safer.

The agency will charge you a fee, usually a percentage of the first month's salary, or a flat rate. Make sure you have an idea of how much they are likely to charge you before you start.

Check whether they are likely to be able to fill the position from those on their books at present; if they are not, there may be advertising charges on top. Also check what happens if they recruit someone who doesn't work out. Most offer some sort of rebate, on a sliding scale, during the first few months of employment. This, and the fact that a properly briefed and competent agency can sift down to a tight shortlist, can make what initially seems an expensive way of doing things more attractive.

To get the best from them, you will still need to do a lot of the groundwork. If you don't know what you want, they won't be able to help you find it. So go along armed with:

- the job title and a brief description of the duties;
- your employee specification;

- an idea of how much you are prepared to pay the person selected, plus any other relevant terms and conditions;
- a view on how much you want the agency to do, and how much you are prepared to do yourself – in terms of shortlisting and interviewing;
- your questions about their method of operation and charging, and how long they think it will take to fill your vacancy.

METHODS OF APPLICATION

Whichever source of recruitment you are using, it pays to plan how candidates should apply, and how you will deal with them when they do. There are six main options, each with advantages and disadvantages.

Candidates call in person, perhaps on a specified day

This may be the quickest solution – but, unless you have briefed the Job Centre or agency very thoroughly, there will be no chance to sift out the patently unsuitable.

You can, of course, ask candidates to complete an application form on arrival. Unless the job requires a reasonable level of written skill or form filling, you should be prepared to help those who have difficulty completing it – especially anyone whose mother tongue is not the language on the form.

Application forms in general provide a good and systematic way of gathering information to assess suitability. By asking candidates to sign to confirm the accuracy of the information they supply, you can also safeguard yourself against fraudsters. If you discover after you have taken a candidate on that this information was false, you should be able to dismiss them without fear of legal retribution.

Asking people to complete an application form may seem a bit bureaucratic, but a relatively simple one like that overleaf is quite quick and easy to fill in. You can get copies from Chancellor Formecon (see Useful Addresses, p. 45).

Candidates telephone for a preliminary discussion

This is another quick way to check an application, but you will need someone capable of conducting a telephone interview to answer calls (see Chapter 5) and you will still need some written details later.

Candidates telephone for an application form

This takes longer, and means some applicants may lose interest, especially those for jobs that do not normally involve much paperwork. It does, however, enable you to consider applications at your convenience.

Candidates write, enclosing a curriculum vitae (CV)

With this system it will be several days before you see any response to your advertisement. Those who are seriously looking for a professional or managerial job will probably have their CV typed up and ready to hand. Those who were simply attracted by your advertisement may be deterred by the need to prepare one. Candidates for less specialist jobs will almost certainly be put off.

CVs also have the disadvantage that the candidate tells you what they want to tell you – rather than precisely what you need to know. This can make it harder to assess how well they really match your specification.

Candidates write to explain how they meet the requirements

This method will be easier for those not accustomed to preparing their CV. However, unless you subsequently ask for an application form to be completed, you are likely to obtain only partial information about the candidate's background – the part they want to know. It will often be hard to assess much beyond handwriting skills and the capacity to write a business letter – neither of which may be particularly relevant to the job to be filled.

Candidates write for an application form

This is also relatively slow but, once the completed forms arrive, you will be able to compare similar information about each candidate, against your specification.

Whichever method you choose, bear in mind the candidates' convenience and expectations as well as your own. This is equally important when you move on to set up your selection procedure.

PRIVATE & CONFIDENTIAL

APPLICATION _Concise Form_
FOR EMPLOYMENT
Please return completed form to:

APPLICANT Please complete in INK using BLOCK CAPITALS

Forename(s)	
Surname	
Previous Surname(s)	
Home Address	
	Postcode

Position applied for

Enclosed with this Application form _(tick as applicable)_
- [ ] Job Description
- [ ] Occupational Health Assessment / Screening Questionnaire _(Pre-employment)_

Employment Place(s) of work [ ] At address given above
- Full-time | Part-time &/or [ ]
- Permanent | Temporary

Tel. No. (home)	
E-mail address (home)	
Tel. No. (work)	
Date of Birth	/ /
If you are shortlisted, you will be asked to produce a 'specified document' (e.g. a P45, NINO card, UK or Eire birth certificate, passport) confirming your eligibility to live and work in the UK in accordance with the Asylum and Immigration Act 1996 - Section 8.	
Would you be able to produce such a document ?	YES / NO
Would you have to move home if offered this job ?	YES / NO
Do you have a current clean driving licence ?	YES / NO
For what classes of vehicle ?	

OPTIONAL QUESTIONS in this shaded area. _Please see declaration on reverse_

Ethnic Origin
For the purpose of monitoring census data, please indicate the ethnic group to which you belong. Ethnic origin is not about nationality, place of birth or citizenship; it concerns colour and broad ethnic group.
(tick box)
- [ ] White
- [ ] Bangladeshi
- [ ] Indian
- [ ] Pakistani
- [ ] Black African
- [ ] Black Caribbean
- [ ] Black Other _(specify)_
- [ ] Chinese
- [ ] Other Asian (state)
- [ ] Other (state)

No. of penalty points (if any) endorsed on current driving licence

Have you ever had your driving licence revoked ? YES / NO

Your living accommodation, e.g. owner occupied house, rented flat, living with parents

GENERAL EDUCATION

Secondary Education			Further Education		
From	To	Name of school	From	To	Name of college, university etc.
/	/		/	/	
/	/		/	/	

Examination results/qualifications obtained

EMPLOYMENT

Name and address of current employer _(or last employer if not currently employed)_	Job title and main duties	Employment Dates	
		From	To
		/	/

Average gross pay £ _____ per week / month / annum   Reason for leaving

Previous employment _(employer name and your job title)_	Job title			
1			/	/
2			/	/
3			/	/

HEALTH

Height	Weight	Would you be willing to have a medical examination if required ? YES / NO

OPTIONAL QUESTIONS in this shaded area. _Please see declaration on reverse_

Do you smoke ? YES / NO _(if YES, give details of past and present tobacco usage)_   Are you currently receiving any medical treatment ? YES / NO _(if YES, give details)_

Note: If we have sent you a separate Occupational Health form, please complete and post it to the Medical Advisor in an envelope marked 'Strictly Private & Confidential'.
(Note to Employer - see Chancellor Formecon form ref. FS.25)

47

attracting **talented people**

PRACTICAL SKILLS

Summarise job skills acquired and specialist training received

What qualities do you have which most suit you to the job you are applying for?

GENERAL

What are your main interests, sports and hobbies?

To which clubs or societies do you belong?

Do you have any other employment (including any part-time work) which you intend to continue? YES / NO *If YES, give details*

Do you have any other commitments which may limit your working hours, e.g. judicial, military or local government? YES / NO *If YES, give details*

Future training plans (give details of any courses you intend to pursue)

Have you ever been dismissed from employment? YES / NO *If YES, give reason*

Have you ever been convicted of a criminal offence? (NB. The Rehabilitation of Offenders Act 1974) YES / NO

Please give any other information relevant to your application, e.g. outline any notable achievements

REFERENCES

Names and addresses of two referees

Work Experience

| | Tel.No. | | Can they be contacted now? YES / NO |

Character

| | Tel.No. | | Can they be contacted now? YES / NO |

AVAILABILITY

When would you be available for interview?

If offered this job when could you start?

Do you have any leave (holiday) commitments?

How did you hear about this job?

Do you know anyone in our employment? (give names)

If you require space for additional information, please enter below

This application form was completed by: *(tick appropriate)*	
Applicant only	
Applicant with some assistance	
Someone other than applicant	

DECLARATION Please read carefully, then sign and date your application

I confirm that the information I have provided is correct and understand that misleading statements may be sufficient grounds for cancelling any agreements made. I also understand that questions left unanswered may be discussed at interview(s) arising from this application.

Applicant signature	Date
	/ /

FOR OFFICE USE ONLY

This form is reproduced with the permission of the copyright holder and publisher, Chancellor Formecon, Crewe.

assessing **potential** 5

SELECTING APPLICANTS FOR INTERVIEW

However many applications you receive, and in whatever form, your starting point when assessing them must be your employee specification (see Chapter 3). If you lose sight of this, you risk taking on someone who looks and/or sounds good, but who lacks some of the essential knowledge and skills that make the difference between success and failure in the job. You are also far more likely to allow yourself to be ruled by your prejudices – the dangers of which have already been discussed.

Handling telephone replies

If you have asked candidates to ring for an application form, all you need is someone to answer the phone, write names and addresses on envelopes, and insert the form ready for posting. If, however, you have asked candidates to phone for a preliminary discussion, you will need to prepare for this in the same way as you would for any other interview.

Have a checklist of relevant questions ready by the phone. Note each caller's replies on a separate sheet of paper, headed with their name, address, daytime and home telephone number. If you do decide to take their application further, this will at least ensure you know where to contact them. The notes of the conversation will have the added advantages of helping you plan a more formal interview later and of ensuring that you have a record of what was said: this is important in case anyone subsequently claims that you turned them down because of their race, sex, marital status or disability.

Your main aim at this stage is to identify those candidates whom you are interested in seeing – and who are interested in seeing you. Don't try to cover every point, but select three or four key requirements, and see what the candidate has to offer. For example:

- If your advertisement stated that you needed particular technical or professional knowledge and skill, remind callers of this, and ask them to give you examples of when and where in their previous work experience or educational background they may have developed these skills

- Explain that you need someone who is a good planner and organiser (if this is the case) and ask them to tell you about an instance where they proved themselves to be both

- If you need someone who is comfortable working on their own, ask them what the set–up was in their previous job(s) and how they enjoyed it

- If a pleasant telephone manner, clear speaking voice or articulate presentation are requirements of the job, note how the candidate matches up. Particular accents or dialects are less important than the ability to make yourself understood in an assertive, but not aggressive, manner

- Ask the candidate what else, if anything, they feel they need to know at this stage. You don't want to invite a torrent of detailed questions, but you do need to make sure the candidate stays interested.

Selecting different questions for different jobs is likely to prove a more fruitful line of enquiry than simply asking people to rattle off a list of previous employers, job titles and qualifications.

However, this approach does presuppose that the person conducting the interview is able to think of sensible follow-up or clarifying questions and to answer routine questions from the candidates. They may not need to evaluate candidates' replies in much detail, though – depending on whether you want to let people know the outcome then and there. Time permitting, there are advantages in waiting until you have a clearer picture of the size and quality of the response before issuing invitations to interview.

Either way, the conversation should end with thanks to the candidate for taking the time to call, and a clear indication of what will happen next.

Handling written replies

Again, you must know what you are looking for. If you need someone who expresses themselves clearly in writing, who will have to complete printed forms as part of their work, or who can spell correctly, it will be relevant to consider these aspects of their letter, form or CV. If the job will involve none of these things, concentrate on what they say (about their education, employment and practical skills) instead. You are looking for indications that candidates have, or have not, developed the knowledge and skills you need.

Some applications – the ones from people who are doing a similar job elsewhere – will stand out and should probably go on your pile of people to see. Check first, though, that their reason for leaving their present employer is sound. The fact that they were sacked doesn't automatically rule them out, but it won't take them to the top of the pile either. If they are looking for more money, promotion, or more responsibility, can you provide this? If not, there's not much point in going any further.

Others contenders are likely to be less obvious, for various reasons. They will be the ones whose practical skills appear to match those you seek, but whose employment or educational record leads you to wonder whether they are really up to your standard. If the 'to see' pile is looking a bit sparse, you will want to add the best of these to it, to find out how strong the candidate really is.

However, you should resist the temptation to add people you are doubtful of to the 'to see' pile. Even the most rudimentary interview will take fifteen minutes or so, and you will need an hour or even longer to do a thorough job – so one of the main purposes of this exercise is to keep the 'to see' pile to a manageable number.

Excluding applicants – some considerations

- Unless the response has been very poor, exclude anyone who hasn't provided enough detail to allow you to assess whether or not they match your requirements, or anyone who lacks an essential requirement – such as a clean driving licence for a job involving driving

- Also reject those who indicate that they won't be available for interview or to start work when you need them, and those who indicate that they have other commitments that would prevent them fulfilling the demands of the job.

- People over the state retirement age (now 65 for both men and women) can continue working if they wish, but there are tax implications that they should check out. Children under the age of thirteen cannot legally be employed at all, and the hours that can be worked by young people under sixteen are restricted by law. If any of your applicants fall in this category you will need permission from the local education authority

- It will not be worth considering any applicants who need a work permit, unless the work is very specialised and you have been unable to attract any other suitable candidates from within the European Union. If you think it worth a try, consult the manager of your local Job Centre before proceeding. (It is a criminal offence to employ anyone over the age of sixteen who is subject to immigration control and does not have permission to work.)

- You may prefer to let a larger employer take the risk with people with a poor health record or for whom this will be their first job after a prolonged or serious illness – especially as there are no rebates for the first four weeks of Statutory Sick Pay

- Disabled people are in a rather different category. If you employ more than fifteen people it is illegal unjustifiably to treat a disabled person less favourably than others or to fail to make reasonable adjustments to the work or the workplace that would enable a disabled person to do the job. If you have any queries about employing a disabled person, contact the Disability Employment Adviser at your local Job Centre or seek out your local Placing Assessment and Counselling Team (PACT)

- Do not automatically rule out those who admit to having been convicted of a criminal offence. If the offence was relatively minor (i.e. one that led to probation more than five years ago, or a prison sentence that was less than 30 months long and more than 10 years ago), it may well be what the Rehabilitation of Offenders Act, 1974 describes as 'spent'. That means it is illegal for you to take the offence into account when making your decision

- And even if it is more serious or more recent, much will depend on the nature of the offence and of the work to be done. You would be foolhardy to employ a convicted embezzler to handle your accounts, unless you were very sure that they had been successfully rehabilitated. Employing them as a chef or a technician might be less risky.

Once you have got a manageable 'to see' pile, you can start notifying the unsuccessful applicants. Unless you are very confident that you will find the right person among those you plan to see, it may be a good idea to keep one or two of the 'nearly possibles' on hold until after the next stage in your selection procedure.

THE INTERVIEW

If you asked candidates to apply in person, you may already have a queue of people waiting at your door. If, on the other hand, you asked people to write or telephone for an application form or to take part in a telephone interview, you have a little time to plan how best to approach the interview itself.

Planning the interview

The first task is to decide where to hold the interview. If you are recruiting unskilled labour and your specification is very basic, you can talk to people on the building site or the shop floor. If you need anything more than physical strength and a reasonable level of reliability, you really need somewhere to talk in a bit of peace and privacy for at least part of the time.

It can be difficult to follow the thread of what a candidate has to say if you are constantly being interrupted by the telephone, customers, other employees or the sound of machinery. You may want to make sure your preferred candidates have a chance to see where they would be working later on, and to get the feel of the place – but that can wait.

If you don't have anywhere suitable, and are seeing a number of candidates, the local Job Centre may be able to let you have a room. Alternatively, you could meet candidates at your premises and then take them out for a coffee, if there's somewhere local. As a last resort, but only if there is no other alternative, you could conduct interviews in your car or van, although you must make sure you are parked where people can see you, for your own protection. Such a cramped setting is far from ideal, however; you really need to sit where you can relax a bit and see each other clearly.

Once you have decided the location, you must give candidates clear information about the date, time and place of the meeting and tell them how to find you and who to ask for. You can now give some serious thought to the questions you would like answered.

You have two equally important goals in the interview:

- to determine whether the candidate is right for the job;
- to determine whether the job is right for the candidate.

Recruiting someone who isn't capable of doing the job you want done can be expensive for you, as was discussed in Chapter 1. But it's no use recruiting someone who doesn't want this sort of job, in your sort of company. They won't give of their best, and may not last long: your aim must therefore be to paint as clear a picture as possible of what is involved, so that there will be no nasty surprises later.

Tips for successful interviews

Keep your employee specification firmly in mind If you haven't already put your requirements into order of priority, do so now. Are there any sensible trade-offs you can make? For example, could you settle for someone who isn't that creative, provided they really are good at getting the best out of other people? This will help you decide the order of your questions and how much time you wish to devote to each area.

Think how best to word your questions

Open questions – like 'how', 'how many', 'how often', 'what', 'with what results' – will take you further than direct or yes/no questions. Instead of asking 'Did you enjoy your last job?' – which invites a 'Yes' or 'No' in reply – try 'What was it about your last job that you enjoyed most?' This forces the candidate to think and to be specific.

Be ready to probe

React to answers with more open questions: 'What factors influenced you?'; 'What happened then?'; 'How did your boss react to that?'; 'What was the customer's response?'

Plan the content

Unless the candidate has failed to provide clear answers to the questions on the application form, don't be tempted to spend a lot of time going through it. You may want to check the sequence of jobs and reasons for moving – to see whether the pattern that emerges is one of a feckless wanderer, an ambitious self-seeker, or a logical progression. You may also want to investigate any gaps in the sequence – which could hide a period of illness, unemployment, moonlighting or a spell in prison not declared on the form. Beyond that, simply retracing their steps will take too long and take the focus away from the attributes you are looking for.

For the same reason, aim to keep the discussion as practical as possible. People who wish to expound their theory of the meaning of life may be entertaining in the pub, but in an interview you need hard evidence of what they can and can't do.

Always request specific examples

Don't just ask whether the candidate has or hasn't done, does or doesn't enjoy something. Wherever possible, ask for specific examples, even a practical demonstration. (There are some ideas on the latter in the next section.) Follow up answers with 'Can you give me an example of that?' or 'Could you tell me about a particular instance?'

Never settle for generalisations

Answers like 'Oh yes, I'm very used to dealing with the public' or 'I've got lots of experience of managing complex projects' get you nowhere. Ask 'Can you tell me about a specific occasion when you found a member of the public particularly difficult?... What exactly happened?' or 'What is the most complex project you've managed in the last year?... Tell me precisely how you handled it.' You will find that by using words like 'specific', 'exact' or 'precise' you can get the candidate to focus rather than waffle.

Aim to get a balanced view

If the candidate has given you an example of a customer who was clearly satisfied, ask 'Can you think of a time when a customer didn't go away happy?... Tell me about that.' If you have talked about a project that clearly met its objectives, ask 'Can you think of one that didn't go so well?'

Anticipate the candidates' likely questions

Such questions can vary from specifics like 'When would you want me to start?' or 'How much holiday would I get?' to broader issues such as 'What sort of prospects are there if I show I can do this job?' Your answers will have to be factual: you are expecting the candidate to be precise and honest – you must be too.

Be alert to unspoken clues

To a certain extent, of course, we all judge each other on first impressions, but in an interview you cannot make assumptions: someone who is very thin doesn't necessarily have AIDS or anorexia; shaky hands are no proof of drug abuse; sweating palms or bloodshot eyes do not mean the candidate is an alcoholic. By the same token, you cannot assume that anyone with none of these symptoms is clear of problems.

Although there is no reason why you should not employ someone with a drink, food or drugs problem, or someone who is HIV-positive, you may think there are risks (of erratic performance or frequent absence) associated with these conditions that you would rather not run. If so, you need to be aware of some of the possible signs in the interview: the indications of a drink problem, for example, are usually more subtle than a candidate staggering in reeking of drink.

What you can do is to ask specific questions such as 'How many times in the last year have you been late for work?' or 'Have you missed work (or been unable to get out) for any reason other than those shown on your application form?' If you are really concerned, you can be even more direct – 'There are a few direct questions, not on the application form, which I ask everyone. Have you ever, or do you now, use drugs of any kind? How often do you drink alcohol? Have you ever been breathalysed?'

Such questions will not produce conclusive answers, and you may upset a few genuine candidates by asking them. You must weigh up the risks. If you don't ask the candidate, you may still be able to check with their referees later (see the next section) or ask them to undergo a medical examination.

Don't delve into candidates' private lives

You are interested in a candidate's ability to do the job – to the required standard, usually for a specified number of hours. If a woman happens to disclose that she has young children at home, don't demand to know who looks after them or what happens when they're sick. Instead make it very clear what demands the job will make, and ask for evidence that she can and will satisfy them.

This will obviously be easier if she is already working somewhere else. You can ask her about her attendance record. If she is hoping to come back to work for the first time since having children, you can ask what difficulties she believes she may face in meeting your requirements. As long as your requirements are reasonable, and not trumped up to deter her, you can form a judgement as to whether she is, or is not, likely to fulfil them.

Be consistent and impartial

The same sort of rules apply generally. Try to make sure you follow a similar line of questioning with all candidates. Never ask 'men only' or 'women only' questions. Even if you believe that 'a woman's place is in the home', do not impose this belief on others. Even if the last member of an ethnic minority group you employed walked off with your takings, don't assume that everyone from the same group is likely to do the same. If you are worried about honesty, check it out for everyone, not just those you mistrust. To do otherwise lays you open to claims of sex and race discrimination. It also means you could miss out on some very capable potential employees as a result of sheer blind prejudice.

Be prepared to listen

Leave telling the candidate about your business successes and your expansion plans until later. There is no point identifying all that you need to know about the candidates and then spending half the interview talking about yourself. Give them time to think. Nod and look encouraging when they pause – don't interrupt or jump in with another question. Make notes if you can, perhaps using a copy of your specification as a framework.

Check that you have understood

Every now and then try to summarise what the candidate has said, and then check out any areas that aren't clear. This should help you to avoid getting side-tracked and to remember what was said.

FURTHER CHECKS BEYOND THE INTERVIEW

The guidelines above should help you uncover a lot of information about your candidates – information that should all relate to your employee specification. However, before you attempt to make a decision, there may be a few more specific areas you want to double-check.

There are four basic ways of doing this:

- asking candidates to provide a sample of their work;
- arranging for them to undergo tests;
- taking up references, for some or all of the candidates;
- giving someone a trial before confirming their appointment.

Work samples

The easiest way to check whether prospective delivery drivers can drive your van safely and reliably around your delivery area without getting lost is to ask them to drive you round in the van, perhaps calling in on a few customers on the way (but remember to check their driving licence and your own insurance first). The quickest way to check whether prospective nursery staff know a hydrangea from an azalea and can transplant a shrub without killing it is to walk with them around your garden centre. Have them talk to you about the plants, and ask them to move one or two for you. The simplest way to check whether prospective chefs can make an omelette or a pavlova is to invite them into your kitchen. The best way to check whether prospective designers can take a rain-soaked sketch and turn it into a professional drawing, or whether prospective secretaries can take some scribbled figures and a few notes and turn them into a specification, is to ask them to do it.

All these examples are based on the principle that, if you really want to know whether or not someone is competent to perform key elements of the job to the standards you require, the best way is to let them show you what they can do. This may not prove that those who do perform to the required standard will automatically do so, day in, day out, should you employ them. But it will help you to identify any who simply do not have what it takes.

There are drawbacks, of course. First, if you need candidates to be competent in more than one task, devising and obtaining work samples for each aspect can become very time consuming – for you and the candidate. For you, there may be some compensation if you are able to use the output produced – the omelette, the drawing or the specification – but this will rather depend on the quality of the work. If you overdo it, or fail to explain what you are doing and why, some of your candidates may decide there are easier ways to get a job.

Secondly, if the task is one that requires some initial training – knowledge of your particular products or of the layout of your premises, skill in using a particular machine or familiarity with a particular home-grown system – you will have to spend some additional time teaching candidates the basics. This will be particularly crucial if candidates might otherwise be put at risk. The old building trade ploy of placing a bag of cement on the candidates' chair and expecting them to remove it seems like a good way of assessing whether they have the strength to do the work. It could backfire, though, if someone who had not been trained to lift suffered an injury.

Finally, unless you take plenty of time and care explaining to candidates what is required, you could find you are indirectly discriminating against candidates whose first language differs from your own. Given more time and clear instructions or a demonstration, they may be perfectly capable of performing to the required standard. If you assume they are not, on the basis of a hasty briefing or an ill-devised test, you could lay yourself open to a claim of racial discrimination.

One way of reducing the impact of some of these problems is to ask candidates to bring their own work samples with them. In some fields this is standard practice: graphic designers, for instance, will expect to show a portfolio of their work. The risk here is that you have no way of knowing whether all the contents are genuinely theirs. It is also a problem where work is actually the property of a previous employer.

Work samples give you the chance to judge for yourself what someone is capable of. Even if you and your candidates are prepared to take the time and trouble to use them, there will be aspects of some jobs that cannot readily be assessed by such means. Anything that involves a prolonged period of training, or a significant level of involvement with customers or other employees, will be hard to cover. In such cases, you have three other options: formal tests, references and trial periods.

Formal tests

Psychologists have devised a number of ways of assessing the personality traits, patterns of thought, and mental and physical aptitudes that make us what we are. Such psychometric tests are strictly not for amateurs.

If you are trying to fill a very important or complex job, and don't feel you will be able to assess candidates adequately using the methods so far outlined, try talking to a reputable employment consultant. They should be able to offer you some more sophisticated ways of predicting how candidates are likely to perform. Since most of these require specialist training to administer and interpret, such services do not come cheap.

Nor, of course, are they necessarily much more reliable than a well-constructed interview and work sample. For one–off recruitment assignments it is not easy for consultants to gauge exactly what level of performance on a given test is really needed to meet your requirements. Their assessments will tend to relate to norms for the population at large. The real benefit of such methods tends to come when relatively large numbers of people are recruited and can be followed up over a long period.

References

Some applicants can sound too good to be true. All are likely to be trying hard to put a positive complexion on what they have done. For particularly sensitive areas – like honesty, drink, drugs or other problems – and for those aspects you haven't been able to explore in other ways, references can be a useful source of additional information. Use them either to help you decide, or as a check after you have made up your own mind who is the best candidate.

References from previous employers are of more value than personal or character references. Most people know someone who thinks well of them, though if the referee has some standing in the local community – especially a teacher, doctor or other professional person – they are perhaps less likely to mislead deliberately. If the candidate names someone who is not the immediate past employer as a referee for experience, it is worth asking why. Often this will be because the candidate is still employed and doesn't wish to alert their present boss until another job has been offered. If this is the case, either ask if you can contact their previous boss, or make it clear that any offer of employment will have to be subject to a satisfactory reference from their current employer.

If this subsequently proves unsatisfactory and is received within a reasonable time, you will be able to sack the employee if you want to – although that may not be much consolation if you have just spent time getting them settled in, and it won't be much consolation to them either.

It is not good practice for you to contact referees without the candidate's permission, nor for the candidate to put the names and addresses of referees on the application form, without getting their consent first. Wherever possible, telephone referees with some prepared questions. If contacting a previous employer, try to make sure it is the candidate's immediate boss you are talking to.

Your questions should seek to obtain:

- confirmation of the dates of employment and the nature of the duties performed;
- details of the number of days' absence, and a comment on the candidate's punctuality;
- observations on their work performance and general conduct;
- clarification of their reason for leaving and how likely the employer would be to re–employ them.

If the answers don't tally with the information supplied by the candidate, double-check. Say something like 'That's interesting. I had understood he left you rather more recently than that . . .' or 'You haven't mentioned it, but I understood she did from time to time get involved in handling cash. Is that so?' Make all your questions as specific as you can: 'How accurate was his figure work?' 'How often did you receive complaints from customers?' 'Were there ever any indications of drug or solvent abuse?'

Things to bear in mind when asking for references

- Some employers prefer not to implicate themselves by giving a bad reference

- Some employers will be satisfied with standards of work and conduct a good deal lower than yours

- Some employers will be glad to get rid of a problem employee and may decide to be 'economical with the truth'

- Some employers will have lost their records, forgotten the employee, or muddled them up with someone else.

Be alert for signs of any of these – and be prepared to use your own judgement. Even if someone does mislead you and you suffer as a result, the scope for legal redress is very limited.

Trial periods

However carefully you have approached your selection, you can never be certain. One way round this, which has advantages for you and gives you the chance of an extended work sample, is to offer the job for a trial period. You may decide to withhold service-related sickness benefits, any pension arrangements or other fringe benefits until after the completion of, say, a three-month trial. That may reduce your costs, and make you feel less tied. It should also prompt you to review progress regularly, especially during the first three months, to your mutual benefit.

In practice, trial periods achieve little beyond this. Unless you were acting on the basis of trade union activities, race, sex or disability, you could sack the employee in the first few months in any case without having to prove you were acting reasonably. If the new recruit is to have any real chance of success, you will have to spend some time helping them to get to grips with the job: doing it half-heartedly will be a waste of time for both of you. And a trial period may be quite unappealing for the employee, especially if they are giving up another job to come to you.

Whether or not you think there is merit in proceeding on a trial basis, you are now in possession of as many facts as you are likely to need. You should now be ready to make your decision.

6 **signing** up

REVIEWING THE EVIDENCE

Even if one of your applicants emerges as a clear winner, it will be worth spending a while thinking about all the information you have gathered, to ensure you really do offer the job to the best candidate.

Go back over your employee specification and rate each candidate against each item. You can use a scale from 1 to 5, or 'above/below/meets required standard'. Challenge each rating. On what evidence is it based? Where did you get it from – the application form, the interview, a work sample, references?

Look down the list. If one candidate scores high on, say, five out of six requirements and very low on the sixth, you may be tempted to take a chance. However, if the sixth item is critical to success in the job, you may do better to opt for the person who scores slightly lower across the board but highly on the sixth – as long as they at least meet your standard on each.

Remember, too, that someone who is overqualified can be almost as bad as someone who is underqualified in key areas. Unless you can expand the job to make use of their talents, they may quickly become frustrated.

There is, of course, the possibility that no one meets the required standard. If this should happen, you have two options:

- Settle for the best of a bad lot – and recognise that you will probably have to spend more time training the newcomer than you had bargained for. If the shortfall is in an area that is difficult to improve by training – such as honesty – this is not a wise option to take

- Retrace your steps until you find a better way forward. Was there anyone you rejected along the way who might be worth a second look? Was the advertisement worded as well as it might have been? Was the brief to the Job Centre/agency clear? Was your specification really relevant to the job? Was the job itself clearly defined? Should you rethink the job – or even whether you need someone at all?

Whatever the outcome of your deliberations, make sure you keep a few notes about your conclusions. Use the application form or a separate sheet of paper. Record the key points that helped you to make up your mind about each candidate.

Don't be in too much of a hurry to throw away the paperwork for those who are unsuitable. There is just a chance one of the applicants, or someone acting on their behalf, may want to challenge your decision on grounds of race, sex or disability discrimination. Such a challenge will be much easier to refute if you have clear notes, made at the time of selection, recording your reasons for rejection. Clear them out every twelve months, unless you want to keep them on file for a future vacancy, if your first choice fails to match up to your expectations.

CONTACTING THE CANDIDATES

Assuming you are now clear about who best matches your specification, you need to decide whether to telephone, write, or make an offer on the spot.

There is no need to waste time writing for jobs that are typically paid by the hour or the week: use the phone instead. You will have to put all the details on paper soon anyway, and you don't want to risk losing your chosen candidate. For other jobs, too, a phone call gives a sense of being wanted and can get the relationship off to a good start. However, candidates may want you to confirm the details in writing before giving notice to their present employer. The next section will help you to decide what the terms of the offer should be, and how to capture them in a written statement.

As soon as you have an acceptance – but not before – contact any candidates who are still waiting to hear from you and thank them for their time and trouble. You may want to employ one of them at a later date, so try to leave things on a positive footing.

THE TERMS OF THE OFFER

You are about to make an offer that will form the basis of a legally binding contract of employment, when accepted. You need, therefore, to be clear that any promises you make must be honoured, or you will be in breach of contract. It makes no real difference whether the promises are made in writing or speech: things you said at interview or in your advertisement also count, although written promises are, of course, easier for an employee to prove.

To start with, you will need to be clear who you are. This sounds obvious, but it is important that the employee knows who they are actually working for. If you have registered a number of different companies, which is the relevant legal entity? For similar reasons, make sure you have got the employee's name right, to avoid confusion.

There will be at least ten main terms to be covered in the job offer, and others that you may feel important to get straight from the outset. Thinking about them all now will help to make sure you don't put anything in the offer that you don't really mean.

Job title and main duties
You need to be reasonably specific about what you want the employee to do. If the job title is self-explanatory, there is probably no need to elaborate. If there is room for interpretation, a very brief list of the main types of activity involved – e.g. 'cleaning and general workshop maintenance' – should be enough. If you have followed the guidance in Chapter 3, this should be easy.

Place of work

Where is the job based (assuming it is based in one location)? If you need the employee to work in different locations or to travel in the course of their work, what is involved? Will they use their own car or a company vehicle for this purpose? Who is responsible for insurance, maintenance, fuel costs, etc.? What is the procedure for handling expenses? If the employee will work outside the UK for more than one month a year, you will need further details of the relevant terms and conditions.

Start date

If you offer employment, and hence payment, from a certain date, and then postpone this start date – you may have to pay compensation. Take particular care around bank holidays. Don't accidentally start someone on Christmas Day, or you may have to pay for the whole holiday before they've actually done any work at all.

Try not to choose a date when you or other key staff will be too busy to spend a little time with your new recruit. Agree the date with the employee, and allow time to serve appropriate notice with the present employer.

Date on which continuous employment begins

This will only differ from the start date if your new employee worked for an associated company or one you have just acquired.

If the employment is intended to be temporary, make sure that this is clearly stated. If employment is due to end on a fixed date, spell out what this is. If there is a trial period involved, how long will this be, and are there any conditions relating to it?

Rate of pay and pay interval

You must decide whether to pay in cash, by giro or credit transfer, weekly or monthly, and what the basis of calculation is to be. Will you be paying in advance or in arrears?

In the larger small businesses, the trend is towards monthly payment by credit transfer – which is safer and easier than cash, unless you are a cash business. The basis of calculation may be related directly to *output* (so much per piece made or item sold) *or to time worked* (so much per hour, day, week or year) with or without premium payments for overtime. You can, of course, combine the two, and may decide in addition to pay either an individual or group bonus related to sales or profit.

Try to avoid over–complicating the calculation and bear in mind that too much emphasis on 'pounds for effort' can eventually mean that people are reluctant to put in any extra effort without the promise of extra pounds. Equally, too much emphasis on 'pounds for output' can lead to a 'quantity not quality' mentality, which may not be what your customers want.

Your new employee must be offered terms that meet, or exceed, the national minimum wage and reward both sexes equally for work of equivalent value. These terms should also be compatible with those enjoyed by your existing employees; they will probably be what mostly determines the actual level of pay you offer as well. If the post is a specialist one, you may need to gauge the local going rate by looking at advertisements for equivalent positions in the local paper, or by consulting the manager of your Job Centre.

Hours of work

Try to be as specific as possible. This will be quite straightforward if you have a standard working week but, if you are going to ask the employee to work to the flexible or annual hours arrangements discussed in Chapter 2, you will need to let them know how this works.

Bear in mind that those who have worked for you for more than one month, and whose employment will be for more than three months, will be entitled to a guarantee payment for days when you are unable to provide work for them. Although this only applies for five days per quarter, and there is a legal maximum payable, it is better to err on the side of caution. If you will normally need someone for 30 hours per week but may occasionally need them for 35, make sure the offer makes it clear that 30 hours is the norm.

Holiday entitlement

This, too, will have to be compatible with any arrangements you have made for other employees. Does the business close down entirely at certain times?

If an employee wants to take some time as holiday, whose permission must they seek? How much notice do they have to give, and are there any restrictions on the timing of holidays? You can state that no holiday may be taken in the month before Christmas or at the height of the tourist season (or whenever your peak trading periods are). Does your trade or service require cover over bank holidays? You can also decide how much leave the employee may take at once, so as to safeguard the efficient operation of your business.

If you want to vary these arrangements in the future, you will need to give appropriate advanced notice.

Entitlement to sick pay and pensions

If these are to form part of the terms and conditions of your new employee, you must make the basis clear from the outset. The employee must, for example, be told the rules governing the reporting of sickness or other absence. You must also let them know whether the employment is covered by a pensions contracting–out certificate.

Length of notice

The amount you must give to the employee is laid down by law; the amount they must give you nominally follows the same pattern of one week for each year of service up to twelve weeks. In practice, it is usually impossible to enforce more than one month's notice from employees, though many contracts for senior managers do specify longer. If you think you might want to pay in lieu of notice when the employee leaves, make your decision now and reflect it in the joining documentation. If the employees leaving have access to company secrets, or direct contact with customers, it is often a good idea to make a clean break as soon as they are no longer committed to your business.

Details of any relevant collective agreements

If you have entered into any agreement with a trade union that affects the terms and conditions of this employment, you must advise the employee.

If you employ more than 20 people, you will also have to have written details of your disciplinary rules and disciplinary and grievance procedures (the companion volume, *Your People – an employers' guide to successful people management* has more on this).

OFFERING THE JOB

An offer letter that included all the terms outlined above would be very legalistic and possibly off-putting: it is best to write something much briefer and more welcoming. Include everything that you think may influence the candidate to accept – but, if some areas are still open to negotiation, invite your prospective employee to call in to discuss them.

As a guide, the job title, hours, place of work and an indication of the pay and main benefits ought usually to be mentioned. You can either suggest a start date or ask the employee to telephone to agree one. Make it clear that you very much hope they will decide to accept; invite them to call you with any queries or worries – and to confirm their acceptance.

Tell them, either in the letter or when they call, about anything you want them to bring with them when they start work: tools, birth certificate, P45, bank account details, etc. If you provide any workwear or uniform, check their size and get it ordered. You will also need to let them know when and where to report on their first day and maybe even details, like what to wear or where to park.

If the employee does try to negotiate an improvement in the terms you have offered, you will need to be clear how far you are prepared to go. Don't risk upsetting your existing employees, but do look for ways of reaching a mutually acceptable solution.

You want the new recruit to join in a positive frame of mind.

Once the terms are agreed, you should record them all in a *Statement of Employment Particulars.*

You can use the pro forma shown overleaf – obtainable from Chancellor Formecon at the address on page 80. You don't have to give this to the employee before they start work, but anyone whose employment will last for more than one month is entitled to both a principal and a supplementary statement like those shown. Since these must be issued within two months of the beginning of employment, getting the paperwork organised from Day 1 – or before – will save time later. (Any subsequent changes must be notified, in writing, within one month of coming into effect.)

Contract of Employment
Terms & Conditions

Principal Statement of
Employment Particulars

Part

The Employment Rights Act 1996,
The Working Time Regulations 1998

of 2

EMPLOYER'S NAME and ADDRESS

EMPLOYEE'S NAME and ADDRESS

The following are particulars of your contract of employment as at   Date

Place of work is the same as above address   *   Employee Ref.

COMPLETE ALL SECTIONS

Where no particulars apply, state accordingly

Place of work if different
(or state "Various" if employee is required or permitted to work at various places)

Note 1a applies   *   Boxes marked with ★ - enter YES or NO

Note 1b applies   *   See Notes overleaf

Employment began (date)   Continuous employment began (date)
(If any employment with a previous employer is included)

Period employment expected to continue
(If employment not established)   Expiry date
(If employment is for a fixed term)

JOB TITLE
(state title of job employed to do)

Note 2 applies   *

REMUNERATION
(state scale or rate of remuneration, or method of calculation and the intervals at which the remuneration is paid).
Note that remuneration is regarded as more than simply basic pay, and includes other payments, e.g. commission, bonuses and shift pay.

Note 3a applies   *

Note 3b applies   *

Note 3c applies   *

HOURS OF WORK
(state any terms and conditions relating to hours of work, including any terms and conditions relating to normal hours of work)

Note 4a applies   *

Note 4b applies   *

Note 4c applies   *

Note 4d applies   *

HOLIDAYS AND PAID HOLIDAY ENTITLEMENT
(state holidays including public holidays and holiday pay. The particulars given must be sufficient to enable entitlement, including any entitlement to accrued holiday pay on the termination of employment, to be precisely calculated).

Note 5a applies   *

Note 5b applies   *

Note 5c applies   *

When any of the above particulars change, the employer will, not later than one month after the change, provide
a written statement containing particulars of the change.

Signature for
and on behalf
of EMPLOYER

I have read, understand and accept the above particulars and applicable notes overleaf

Signature
of EMPLOYEE

Date   Date

Contract of Employment
Terms & Conditions

Supplementary Statement of
Employment Particulars

*The Employment Rights Act 1996;
The Working Time Regulations 1998*

Part **2** of 2

EMPLOYER'S NAME and ADDRESS   EMPLOYEE'S NAME and ADDRESS

The following are further particulars of your contract of employment as at | Date   Employee Ref.

COMPLETE ALL SECTIONS Where no particulars apply, state accordingly.   See Notes overleaf.   Boxes marked with ✱ enter YES or NO

SICKNESS and/or INJURY		Note 6a applies ✱
(State any terms and conditions relating to incapacity for work due to sickness or injury, including any provision for sick pay. Alternatively, attach a document which gives the particulars or state where such a document can be reasonably accessed by the employee)		Note 6b applies ✱
		Note 6c applies ✱

PENSION ARRANGEMENTS		A contracting-out certificate is in force for this employment. ✱
(State any terms and conditions relating to pensions and pension schemes. Alternatively, attach a document which gives the particulars or state where such a document can be reasonably accessed by the employee)		

LENGTH OF NOTICE

(State the length of notice the employee is obliged to give and entitled to receive to terminate the contract of employment, or enter 'see Collective Agreements below', or enter as statutory minimum')

You are obliged to give your employer the following length of notice to terminate your employment   *See Note 7*

You are entitled to receive from your employer the following length of notice to terminate your employment   *See Note 7*

DISCIPLINARY RULES & PROCEDURES

(State any disciplinary rules and procedures applicable and the manner in which any application should be made if dissatisfied with any disciplinary decision. Alternatively, attach a document which specifies such rules and procedures or state where such a document can be reasonably accessed by the employee)

The Disciplinary Rules and Procedures form part of your contract of employment (see Note to Employer overleaf) ✱

The person to whom you can apply if you are dissatisfied with any disciplinary decision relating to you is   [State name and/or job title]

GRIEVANCE PROCEDURE   See Note 8

(State the manner in which any application for redress of a grievance should be made and any consequent steps. Alternatively, attach a document which sets out such procedures or state where such a document can be reasonably accessed by the employee)

The Grievance Procedure forms part of your contract of employment (see Note to Employer overleaf) ✱

The person to whom you can apply for the purpose of seeking redress of any grievance relating to your employment is   [State name and/or job title]

COLLECTIVE, WORKFORCE and RELEVANT AGREEMENTS   See Note 9

(State any collective / workforce or relevant agreements which directly affect terms and conditions of employment including, where the employer is not a party, the persons by whom they were made)

When any of the above particulars change, the employer will, not later than one month after the change, provide a written statement containing particulars of the change.

Signature for and on behalf of EMPLOYER

I have read, understand and accept the above particulars and applicable notes overleaf

Signature of EMPLOYEE

Date   Date

INTRODUCING THE NEW RECRUIT

Collect together all the correspondence you have had with your new employee – including the application form, the offer letter (if you sent one) and the statement of employment particulars. These will form the basis of a personal file for the employee. If you wish to summarise this information for easy access, and record other relevant items as they occur, you can use an employee data folder – available from Chancellor Formecon.

Tell everyone about the new appointment – especially those who will be working with, or helping to train, the new recruit.

Plan the first few days/weeks and prepare an induction plan. Even if the job is not complicated, you will need to make sure the newcomer meets everyone and has a chance to find their feet.

There are a few things you must make sure new employees understand from the start:

- the location and use of first–aid equipment and fire extinguishers;

- what to do in the event of a fire;

- other essential safety information – e.g. areas where protective clothing is required, procedure for handling hazardous substances or equipment (if you employ five or more people, you are required by law to have a written health and safety policy and appropriate procedures – and to make sure that these are brought to your employees' attention);

- rules about smoking, time–keeping and breaks, and what to do if taken ill;

- the location of essential facilities – toilets, rest room, where they can eat;

- who will pay them their wages or give them their pay slip, and where and when;

- rules about company property and cash handling;

- customer service and other key work standards;

- any special terminology used.

Even if the employee has done similar work before, your business will have some ways of doing things that are different, some of which may have been discussed in the interview. In any case, talk to your recruit to try to establish the differences. That will help you to focus on the key things they will need to learn.

Try to look at things through their eyes. You may not have many of your working routines committed to paper. Now could be the time to try to compile a few simple checklists or flow charts showing what happens to particular inputs in your processes – information, raw material, etc.

You don't have to do this all yourself. In fact, the people who are closest to each aspect may find it quite illuminating to try to capture exactly what they do, in what sequence, and what happens in the case of rejects or failures. They may even be able to simplify the process before the new recruit gets there. Even if they can't, it will be a lot less bewildering for the newcomer if someone can explain, step by step, how to approach each task.

Decide who can best act as a 'mentor', to help the new employee settle in. You may want to do this yourself, or you may choose to delegate the task to someone who will be working more closely with the newcomer. In this case, you should choose someone who can 'show them the ropes' of both the job and the company, without teaching them bad habits.

SETTING UP THE PAYROLL

With a little forethought, you can make sure the newcomer quickly becomes an effective member of your team. One thing that will really upset them, though, is any slip–up over their pay. There are ways of reducing the chances of this happening.

You should by now have decided whether to pay weekly or monthly, in cash or by giro or credit transfer. You will also have decided the amount and basis of payment. If this recruit is the first person you have actually employed, contact your local Tax Office. Seek their advice and make sure you understand their requirements. Ask for a copy of *The Employer's Guide to PAYE*. Talk through the documentation, and establish whether your tax and National Insurance bill will need to be met monthly or quarterly. (You must also remember to contact your insurance broker and arrange Employers' Liability cover. A copy of the certificate must be displayed in each workplace. This is mandatory from the moment you employ your first person – whether full time or part time.)

Set up a procedure for calculating how much the employee is entitled to in each payment period. If pay is related to hours worked, you may need a signing-in sheet or other means of checking how many hours have actually been put in. If overtime is paid at premium rates, these hours must be calculated separately. If there is a bonus, establish a formula for calculating what has been earned and a means of checking claims. If, for example, a mechanic gets £1.00 per machine on top of basic pay, you need to record how many machines they have fixed this month and hence how much money is due.

If this is their first job, or their earnings will be below the tax threshold, or you are not given a P45, ask your new employee to complete Inland Revenue form P46, and send it to the Tax Office. If they are students in full-time education and are working for you in their holidays, complete Form P38(S) and ask the student to sign it. This must be submitted to the Tax Office as part of your year-end return.

Points relating to payment of new employees

Certificate P45

Parts 2 and 3 of this certificate, which should have been given to them by their previous employer, need to be completed. Send part 3 to your Tax Office and keep part 2 safely: it contains information about previous pay received and tax paid in the year to date.

National Insurance and Income Tax

Make sure you know how much National Insurance and Income Tax to deduct from each payment. The Department of Social Security Contribution Tables will enable you to work out how much National Insurance you and the employee must pay. Current copies of the Inland Revenue's PAYE Tax Tables will help you work out the employee's taxable pay and tax due under PAYE.

Unauthorised deductions

Avoid making any unauthorised deductions from the employee's pay. Apart from PAYE, National Insurance and payments under a court order, it is illegal to make *any* deductions without the employee's written consent. This applies to all employees.

Keep proper records For everyone who earns more than the PAYE threshold, use the official *Deductions Working Sheet (Form P12)* to record:

- the employee's name;
- their tax code;
- their pay;
- the earnings on which National Insurance contributions are payable by the employee;
- the amount of National Insurance and income tax deducted;
- any Statutory Sick Pay (SSP) or Statutory Maternity Pay (SMP) due.

(You will find more on SSP and SMP in *Your People II.*)

At the end of the tax year you will have to complete an end-of-year tax return (*Form P14/60*) for each employee and a summary for all employees on *Form P35*, so keep cumulative totals as you go along.

Remember, though, that if you keep employee records on a computer database you will need to contact the Data Protection Registrar (see Useful Addresses at the back of this book) for a licence under the Data Protection Act.

Arrangements with your bank

Calculate how much you owe the employee, how much must be deducted and therefore how much cash you will need or the amount of the credit transfer to be made. Make the necessary arrangements with the bank.

Itemised pay statement

You should prepare an itemised pay statement for each employee before each pay day. This is a legal requirement if you employ 20 or more people on contracts for more than eight hours per week, and is worth doing to get things on a business-like footing and save misunderstandings. This statement should show:

- employee's name
- date
- period for which payment is made
- National Insurance number (optional)
- tax code (optional)
- bank account number and sort code (for credit transfer)
- basic pay for this pay period, indicating basis of calculation
- allowances and additional payments, with reasons
- total gross pay
- tax deducted
- NI deducted
- pension contribution (if applicable)
- any other *authorised* deductions
- net payment enclosed or at the bank.

Payments to the Inland Revenue

Pay the amounts deducted for National Insurance and tax on the due date and handle other paperwork as instructed by the Inland Revenue. If you are ever in any doubt, contact your local Tax Office for advice.

EXPLAINING THE PAYSLIP TO THE EMPLOYEE

When you hand over your new employee's first payslip, take a little time to make sure they understand what it contains and how the payment has been calculated. This is also a good time to find out how the first week or month has gone, and to see if there is anything else you should be planning to help your newest recruit settle in and succeed.

Having now recruited your team, you will need to manage them successfully, professionally and legally. The companion volume, *Your People 11*, also published by Investors in People UK, provides further help in this area and covers such issues as sick pay, maternity leave, discipline, dismissal and redundancy.

6 useful addresses

Advisory Conciliation and Arbitration Service (ACAS) Regional offices
(Head Office)
Brandon House
180 Borough High Street
London
SE1 1LW
Telephone: 0171 210 3000

British Insurance Brokers Association
BIBA House
14 Bevis Marks
London
EC3A 7NT
Telephone: 0171 623 9043

British Safety Council
70 Chancellors Road
London
W6 9RS
Telephone: 0181 741 1231

British Standards Institution
389 Chiswick High Road
London W4 4AL
Telephone: 0171 629 9000

Central Office of Employment Tribunals
The Eagle Building
215 Bothwell Street
Glasgow
G2 7TS
Telephone: 0141 204 0730

Central Office of Industrial Tribunals
(England and Wales)
19–29 Woburn Place
Russell Square
London
WC1H 0LU
Telephone: 0171 925 5000

Chancellor Formecon
Formecon Services Ltd
Gateway
Crewe
CW1 6YN
Telephone: 01270 500800

Commission for Racial Equality
Regional offices
(Head Office)
Elliot House
10–12 Allington Street
London
SW1E 5EH
Telephone: 0171 828 7022

Confederation of British Industry (CBI)
Regional offices
(Head Office)
Centre Point
103 New Oxford Street
London
WC1A 1DU
Telephone: 0171 379 7400

Data Protection Registrar
Wycliffe House
Water Lane
Wilmslow
Cheshire
SK9 5AX
Telephone: 01625 545700

Department for Education and Employment
Sanctuary Building
Great Smith Street
London
SW1P 3BT
Telephone: 0171 925 5000

(Scotland)
Scottish Office
Education and Industry Department
Victoria Quay
Edinburgh
EH6 6QQ
Telephone: 0131 244 0615

Department of Social Security
Advice Line for Employers
For basic enquiries about:
• National Insurance
• Statutory Sick Pay
• Maternity Pay
Telephone: 0345 143143

Department of Trade and Industry (DTI)
Regional offices
(Head Office)
1 Victoria Street
London
SW1H 0ET
Telephone: 0171 215 5000

European Commission Representation in the United Kingdom
8 Storeys Gate
London
SW1P 3AT
Telephone: 0171 973 1992
Personal callers 10am–4.30pm

For enquiries about
• legislation, funding and VAT
Contact your nearest European Information Centre

Employment Medical Advisory Service At your local Health and Safety Executive Area Office

Employment Service
Porterbrook House
7 Pear Street
Sheffield
S11 8JF
Telephone: 0114 273 9190

Equal Opportunities Commission
Regional offices
(Head Office)
Overseas House
Quay Street
Manchester
M3 3HN
Telephone: 0161 833 9244

Federation of Small Businesses
Regional offices
(Head Office)
32 Orchard Road
Lytham St Annes
Lancashire
FY8 1NY
Telephone: 01253 720911

Financial Times Management
Portland Tower
Portland Street
Manchester
M1 3LD
Telephone: 0161 245 3300

Health and Safety Executive
Area offices
(Head Office)
Rose Court
2 Southwark Bridge
London
SE1 9HS
Telephone: 0171 717 6000

Industrial Society
Regional offices
(Information helpline)
Robert Hyde House
48 Bryanstan Square
London
W1H 7LN
Telephone: 0171 262 2401

Institute of Directors
116 Pall Mall
London
SW1Y 5ED
Telephone: 0171 839 1233

Institute of Personnel and Development
2 Savoy Court
The Strand
London
WC2 0EZ
Telephone: 0181 971 9000

Insurance Brokers Registration Council
Higham Business Centre
Midland Road
Higham Ferrers
Northamptonshire
NN10 8DW
Telephone: 01993 359083

Investors in People UK
7–10 Chandos Street
London
W1M 9DE
Telephone: 0171 467 1900

Open University
Walton Hall
Milton Keynes
MK7 6AA
Telephone: 01908 274066

**Royal Society for the Prevention of
Accidents (ROSPA)**
Regional offices
(Head Office)
Edgbaston Park
353 Bristol Road
Birmingham
B5 7ST
Telephone: 0121 248 2000

Society of Pension Consultants
St Bartholomew House
92 Fleet Street
London
EC4Y 1DG
Telephone: 0171 353 1688

useful **addresses**

useful **addresses**

useful **addresses**

useful **addresses**